WITHDRAWN
FROM THE RECORDS OF THE
MID-CONTINENT PUBLIC LIBRARY

D1303624

746.46 N335
Nelson, Marjorie.
Friendships in bloom

MID-CONTINENT PUBLIC LIBRARY
Antioch Branch
6060 N. Chestnut Ave.
Gladstone, MO 64119

AN

The quilts pictured from left to right are Sammarbeid Er Bare Glede
(Work Together is Always a Joy), Basket of Memories and Serenity.

KANSAS CITY STAR BOOKS

The quilts pictured from left to right are December Night, Ocean of Stars and Rebecca's Flowers.

FRIENDSHIPS
in
BLOOM

ROUND ROBIN QUILTS

BY

MARJORIE NELSON & REBECCA NELSON-ZERFAS

KANSAS CITY STAR BOOKS

MID-CONTINENT PUBLIC LIBRARY
Antioch Branch
6060 N. Chestnut Ave.
Gladstone, MO 64119

AN

MID-CONTINENT PUBLIC LIBRARY

3 0000 12457708 5

DEDICATION

This book is dedicated to our husbands Norman Nelson and Mark Zerfas. It is with their love and support that we are able to continue to explore our passions for quilting. We would like to thank them for being so patient, understanding and supportive. Their encouragement helped us get through all the long hours.

ACKNOWLEDGEMENTS

We would like to thank Doug Weaver and Edie McGinnis of The Kansas City Star, Kansas City, Missouri, for helping us through our journey. We would like to express our appreciation to Bill Krzyzanowski for his wonderful photography and hospitality. Thanks, also, to Vicky Frenkel, the page designer, for adding her artistic touch.

Special thanks to Gerd Villadsen from Molde, Norway, for being our Norwegian liaison and for gathering the quilts from Norway for the photographs.

Thank you Paula Kemperman, Belmont, Michigan, and Ardie Sveadas, Sparta, Michigan, for all of your encouragement and help along the way. Many thanks to Nancy Conrad, Martha Mollema, and Linda Hamel, from Frankfort, Michigan, for being there when we really needed you.

A huge thank you to all of the round robin participants who were willing to share their expertise and quilts so that others could enjoy them. Thank you to everyone who shared in our excitement and made the book a reality. Without the sharing of others this book would not have been possible.

Friendships in Bloom
Round Robin Quilts

By Marjorie Nelson and Rebecca Nelson-Zerfas

Editor: Edie McGinnis
Copy Editor: Judy Pearlstein
Designer: Vicky Frenkel
Photography: Bill Krzyzanowski

All rights reserved.
Copyright © 2003 Marjorie Nelson and Rebecca Nelson-Zerfas
No part of this book may be reproduced, stored in a retrieval system, or transmitted in any form or by any means electronic, mechanical, photocopying, recording or otherwise, without the prior consent of the publisher.

Published by Kansas City Star Books.

First edition.

ISBN: 0-9740009-6-5

Printed in the United States of America by Walsworth Publishing Co., Marceline, Missouri

To order copies, call StarInfo at (816) 234-4636 and say "BOOKS."

Order on-line at www.TheKansasCityStore.com.

 KANSAS CITY STAR BOOKS

TABLE OF CONTENTS

ABOUT THE AUTHORS

Marjorie Nelson started quilting and designing in 1975 as a way to express her creativity. In 1980 Marjorie opened a quilt shop in Beulah, Michigan, and was one of the first people to bring the quilting revival to Northern Michigan. Over the years she has traveled to the United Kingdom and Norway to share her quilting expertise. Her quilts have won numerous awards and have traveled in international exhibits. In 2002, Marjorie and Gerd Villadsen were the curators for the Round Robin exhibit "Women Stitching The World Together" which was held at the International Quilt Festival in Houston, Texas.

Rebecca Nelson-Zerfas learned quilting from her mother, Marjorie. Rebecca has been quilting, designing and teaching since 1980.

In 1998, Rebecca purchased her mother's quilt shop. In 2002, Rebecca renamed the shop after her own design company, "Quilts By The Lake." She is an award-winning quilter who has had quilts in international quilt exhibits and also in a museum collection.

Rebecca lives in northern Michigan with her husband Mark.

Marjorie and her husband Norman, live in Northern Michigan where they have raised seven children.

KANSAS CITY STAR BOOKS

INTRODUCTION

The shores of Lake Michigan attracted many Norwegian immigrants. Among them was Rebecca's great grandfather, Anton Staalesen, from Egersund, Norway. He left Norway when he was 12 years old and took a job on a sailing ship.

After extensive travel, he settled in the bustling seaside village of Frankfort, Michigan. He was drawn to the area by Lake Michigan and Betsie Bay, which reminded him of the ocean and the Norwegian fjords. The area supported fishing and shipping industries, important economic factors in both countries. He also found the climate to be similar to Norway. He built his home on a hill overlooking Betsie Bay and Lake Michigan. Rebecca's parents, Marjorie and Norman Nelson, still live in the 100-year-old house Anton built.

In 1992, Marjorie and Norman decided to take a trip to Norway. While they were in Molde visiting relatives, they found a small quilt shop, "Syskrinet AS," owned by Gerd Villadsen. Fortunately, Gerd spoke English well and they quickly became friends. By the end of the week, Marjorie found herself teaching patchwork at Gerd's quilt shop. There were too many people to fit into one classroom so the class was held in two rooms at the same time. The students all spoke English and everything went smoothly.

In 1998, Marjorie and Rebecca traveled to Houston, Texas, for the International Quilt Market and Festival. There they met with Gerd and a few other ladies from Norway. Marjorie and Rebecca had often thought how exciting it would be to participate in a round robin exchange with another country. One evening they approached the Norwegians with the idea. It wasn't long before they had enough quilters from both countries to make the exchange a reality.

The love of quilting brought together thirty-six people who were willing to participate in the adventure. Eighteen people from each country made center blocks and sent a journal for the participants to add information about themselves. Smaller groups were then formed to work on the tops. Each person created and added a border to five different tops. At the eagerly awaited end of the six months, the new creations were returned to their owners. It was exciting to see the different design styles each quilter had developed.

The round robin exchange was featured in the exhibit "Women Stitching The World Together." In 2002, the public was able to view the exhibit when it was shown in Houston, Texas, at the International Quilt Festival. The exhibit came at a time when the world was still recovering from the events of 9-11. Rebecca and Marjorie found when people have something in common, such as quilting, political, social and economic differences seem to evaporate.

Marjorie and Rebecca have participated in round robin exchanges with quilters from Norway, Switzerland and local quilt groups.

The round robin experience can be very rewarding. It allows you to look within and find the creativity that may have gone unnoticed. You may even step out of your comfort zone and work with fabrics and colors that wouldn't normally appeal to you. In the process, you may discover new friendships and strengthen old ones.

ROUND ROBINS - NORWAY

Anne Marit R. Daviknes

Annrid Nerhus

Gerd Villadsen

Marianna Hatlenes

Ann Karin Myren

Pictured left to right: Kristin Rønning, Britt Gjendem Steinstø, Eli Farstad Jensen, Gerd Villadsen, Karin Bjerke, Anne Grete Nakkenn and Tove Melseter.

ROUND ROBINS - MICHIGAN

Jackie Huizen

Nancy Conrad

Paula Kemperman

Jo Black Danford

Ardie Sveadas

Linda Hamel

Pictured left to right: Rebecca Nelson-Zerfas, Marjorie Nelson, Lois Lewis, Cindy Larson, Emilie Kimpel and Nancy Conrad.

Pictured left to right: Marjorie Nelson, Jan Vandermolen, Susan Rand, Paula Kemperman, Ardie Sveadas and Jackie Huizen

ROUND ROBINS

In this book we have given you basic guidelines for creating round robin quilts. You won't find specific patterns for each quilt. Instead. we have compiled "Quilt Recipes." The recipe allows you to make the quilts as shown in the photos. However, most people tend not to follow recipes. They start with a center and mix and match the borders. We encourage you to experiment with the borders and the recipes. Feel free to deviate from the recipes and add your own special touch.

Ålesund, Norway

Molde, Norway

GETTING STARTED

Find a group of people who are willing to take on this challenge. It is a must to have quilters who can follow guidelines and stay on schedule. Set up the rules. A few things to consider:

1. Decide who will provide the fabric for the borders. It may be better to grant the person who is making the border the freedom to choose what colors and fabrics look best for their design. Perhaps something in their stash will be the perfect piece to complement the center block.

2. Ask the group if they want theme quilts.

3. Have a monthly gathering so everyone except the quilt owner can see the quilt in progress. The owner can leave the room.

4. Determine whether everyone would like to have a journal travel with the quilt.

5. Ask if they would like to send a disposable camera with the quilt. Each person could snap a few photos as they work on the quilt.

ROUND ROBIN GUIDELINES

There are many different plans for round robin exchanges. The basis is simple, you start with a square and each member creates and applies a border to your block.

The following are some basics:

1. Use good quality fabric. This is not the place to use up your bargains.

2. Take pride in your work. Your workmanship is a reflection of you.

3. Be creative and try new ideas.

4. Have your borders turned in on time. When you're late, the next person falls behind schedule and has less time to create.

5. Be considerate of other people's feelings.

6. Designate a special place you will keep the round robin. You don't want to end up with it permanently misplaced.

7. Make sure that you work on it with clean hands.

8. Have fun and relax.

ESTIMATED YARDAGE

It's difficult to give yardage requirements for the quilts and borders. The requirements will change depending on the length of the border needed.

To estimate the individual yardage for pieced borders:

Determine how many total blocks you will need._____

Count how many of each template piece you will need for each block._____

Multiply by the total number of blocks you need._____

Divide the width of the fabric (usually 42") by that number.

This will tell you the number of strips you need._____

Multiply this number by the width of the piece you need to cut._____

You will need that much fabric to make the border.

For plain borders: measure the length of the quilt.

You will want to buy enough fabric to be able to cut the borders on the straight of grain (lengthwise along the selvage). This will help prevent the borders from stretching.

BORDER BASICS & EXTENSION BORDERS

MEASURING THE QUILT FOR BORDERS

Each time you add a border, the quilt must be measured. Find a flat hard surface on which the entire quilt can be spread out. Measure the quilt through the center from edge to edge. Be careful not to stretch the tape measure or the quilt. Cut two borders that length. Sew them to the quilt. Press the seams towards the borders. Measure the quilt again through the center of the quilt from edge to edge. Cut the other two borders this length and sew them to the quilt.

To figure out the length of pieced borders you need, measure the quilt through the center. Find a number that divides evenly into the measurement. Sew the required number of blocks together for one side. Measure the border length. Make sure it is the right length for the quilt. If it's too short, add another block. You will run into problems if you try to stretch the border to make it fit. If the border is too long use an extension border. It's the perfect solution for getting borders to fit properly.

Extension Borders: use them when the eyes need a resting place before the next border is added or to help accentuate the pieced borders. They make your pieced border fit if the border is longer than the top.

To figure out the width of the extension border, you need to:

• Measure the quilt top through the center from edge to edge.

• Measure the pieced border.

• Subtract the quilt length from the border length and divide that number by 2. Add 1/2" to this measurement.

• Cut the extension borders this width by the desired length.

SETTING BORDERS ON POINT:

You can take almost any smaller quilt block and set it on point to make a border. A center square can also be set on point, i.e. the corners are oriented straight up and down rather than straight across from one another.

Formula: corner triangles: divide the finished block size by 1.414 and add 7/8". Cut a square this size. Cut it in half once on the diagonal.

Side triangles: multiply the finished block size by 1.414 and add 1 1/4". Cut a square this size and cut in half twice on the diagonal.

Decimal Equivalents:

1/8" = .125

1/4" = .25

3/8" = .375

1/2" = .5

5/8" = .625

3/4" = .75

7/8" = .875

STRAIGHT OF GRAIN

The straight of grain is very important in quilting. The straight of grain runs lengthwise along the selvage. It has very little stretch. When using templates with arrows, place the arrows on the straight of grain. Borders should also be cut on the straight of grain.

PRESSING

Problems can arise from improper pressing. Some people iron their quilts the same way they iron clothes. This can easily lead to fabric distortion. Instead of ironing, gently press the seams. The seams are usually pressed towards the darker fabric but may be pressed open or toward the lighter fabric if it helps to decrease bulk.

A P P L I Q U É

NEEDLE TURN

Types of thread: everyone has their favorite thread to use. We like "Tire Silk" and "DMC 100% cotton machine embroidery #50 thread". If you have problems with tangling thread, you may want to use a thread conditioner such as beeswax or "Thread Heaven."™

Needles: straw needles work well. You need a long slender needle to effectively turn the fabric.

Seam allowance: add between 1/8" - 1/4" to your templates. It's easier to fold under less fabric. As you start to appliqué you will get a feel for how much seam allowance you need.

Needle turn appliqué: make a knot at the end of the thread. Fold a small length of the seam allowance under. Bring the threaded needle up from the backside and catch a few threads of the folded edge. Take the needle from the top back to the underside. Come up again about 1/8" away from the stitch. Use the end of the needle and tuck under the seam as you appliqué. Repeat the process until you have the piece appliquéd to the background fabric.

Machine Appliqué: cut the templates out of fabric that has fusible web ironed to the underside. Follow the manufacturer's directions on how to use their product. You need to sew around the edges after they are fused in place. Make sure the fusible web you buy allows for this.

Button Hole Stitch: you may use this stitch with a lightweight fusible web.

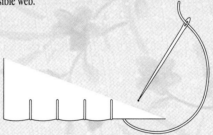

French Knots: Wrap embroidery thread around the needle three times. Take the needle with the thread through the center of the knot to the fabric. Tie off with a knot.

BIAS STRIPS FOR VINES

There are fusible bias tape makers on the market that come in a variety of sizes. This allows you to quickly make the vine and fuse it in place. This is the method we prefer to use.

To make bias tape the old fashioned way:

Decide the finished width that you want and add 1/2". Cut the bias strips on a 45° angle. You want them to be cut on the bias so they will turn easier. Sew them end-to-end until you have enough bias tape. Fold under a 1/4" seam allowance on each long side.

QUILT BINDING

Bias Binding:

Cut 2 3/4" bias strips on a 45° angle. Sew the ends together and press the seams open. Fold the binding in half lengthwise and press. Sew the binding to the top of the quilt. Stop 1/4" from the corner and flip the binding straight away from you.

Then bring it back down facing you. There should be a 45° angle under the binding. Sew the rest of the binding around the quilt.

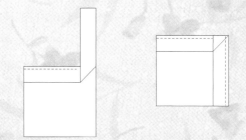

After the binding is sewn to the top, fold it to the back of the quilt and sew it in place by hand.

SQUARING UP THE TOP:

You will need to do this before sending it on to the next person. Make sure the quilt lies flat. If it doesn't, you need to take the time to fix it. This may mean sewing the borders on again. Don't let the next person get your problem. It's also necessary to square it up after you get it from the last person. Each time a quilt is handled, folded, pressed, etc. it can become distorted.

Use the largest square that you can find. We like to use the "Creative Grid"™ 20 1/2" square. It has easy to read marks and has a non-skid back. Place the square in the corner. Take a rotary ruler and place it against the square. Trim away any excess fabric.

BORDER GUIDELINES

The borders are to be added in the following order:

1. Triangle Border: Triangles may be arranged any way you like. Since certain blocks are made of triangles, try to make the border complement the whole.

2. Appliqué Border: When making the appliqué border, make sure you sew around all edges. The pieces may come off or fray if you don't.

3. Plain Border: Add a plain border that isn't any larger than 2" wide finished. You may add a "fancy plain border" if you think it needs to be jazzed up a bit.

4. Border of Squares: Squares may be added in a variety of ways. Squares also make up many types of quilt blocks so be sure the border complements rather than conflicts.

5. Border of Choice: Finish the top in any way that you would like. The border can be pieced or appliquéd. This is your opportunity to make the quilt sing!

FINISHING UP THE QUILT

1. Square up the quilt

2. Layer the backing, batting and the top and baste the layers together.

3. Either hand quilt using small running stitches or quilt by machine.

4. Cut off the excess batting and fabric as you square up the quilt.

5. Apply the bias binding.

6. ENJOY!!!

QUILT RECIPES

STAR IN BLOOM

S T A R   I N   B L O O M

Quilt Created By:

Linda Hamel - Frankfort, Michigan

Nancy Conrad - Frankfort, Michigan

Linda Hamel - Frankfort, Michigan

Rebecca Nelson-Zerfas - Beulah, Michigan

Marjorie Nelson - Frankfort, Michigan

The Quilt Recipe:

Center: "Christmas Star" 12" finished block found on page 16.

Triangle Border: "Sawtooth Star Border" found on page 100.

Plain Border: See instructions on "Extension Borders" found on page 9.

Appliqué Border: "Star Bloom Border" found on page 125.

Triangle Border: "Split Hourglass" using 3" finished blocks found on page 97.

Border of Choice: "Scrappy Rectangles Border" found on page 166.

Quilting has been a surprising and rewarding way of discovering my creative voice. Although participating in the round robin forced me out of my comfort zone, it also opened the door to a new level of confidence and a greater appreciation and enjoyment of my quilting friends.

– Linda Hamel - Frankfort, Michigan

CHRISTMAS STAR

12" Finished Block

Measurements include 1/4" seam allowance.

Cutting Requirements:

Pink fabric: Template B: cut a 4 1/2" square.

Pink fabric: Template E: cut one 5 1/4" square and cut in half twice on the diagonal.

Pink fabric: Template G: cut four 2 7/8" squares and cut in half once on the diagonal.

Background print:

Template D: cut eight 2 1/2" squares.

Template A: cut two 5 1/4" squares and cut in half twice on the diagonal.

Template C: cut two 3 1/4" squares and cut in half twice on the diagonal.

Gold fabric: Template F: cut four 2" squares.

Green fabric: Template G: cut four 2 7/8" squares and cut in half once on the diagonal.

Piecing Guide: Sew the C triangle to F. Make four units. Press the seam allowance towards the square. Sew the other C triangle to the other side of F. Press the seam allowance towards the square. Sew the Green G triangles to this unit. Press the seam allowance towards the green.

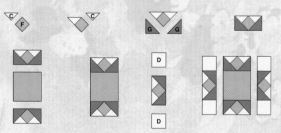

Sew two of these units to the top and bottom of a pink B square. Press the seams towards the square.

Sew background D to both ends of the other two units. Again, press the seam allowance towards the D piece.

Sew these units to the other sides of the block.

Sew triangle A to E. Make four units. Press the seam allowance towards A. Sew triangle A to the other side of E. Press the seam allowance towards A. Sew triangle G to both ends of these units. Press the seam allowance towards G. Sew two of these sections to the top and bottom of the square. Press the seams towards the square. Sew the corner squares to the ends of the remaining sections. Press the seam allowance towards the corner squares. Sew to the sides of the block.

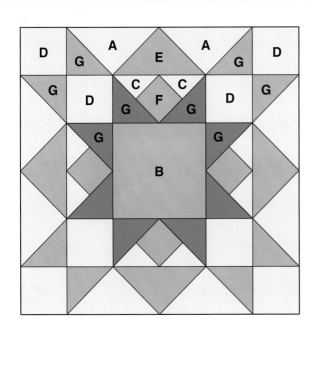

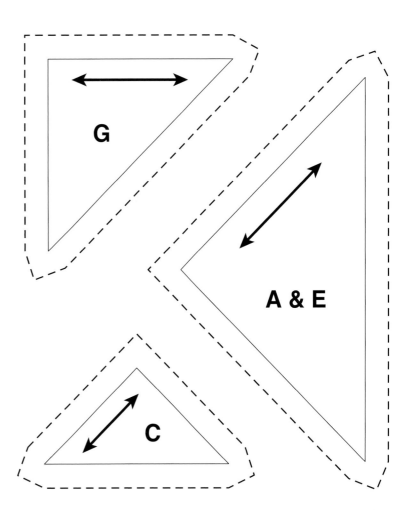

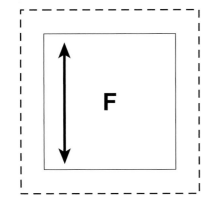

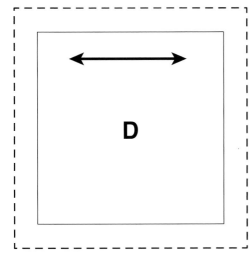

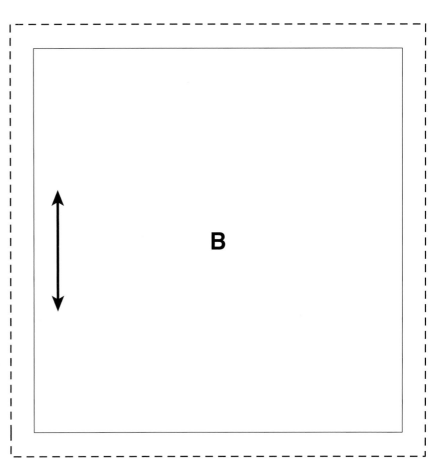

WIND, SAND, AND SKY:
A DAY AT THE LAKE

WIND, SAND, AND SKY:
A DAY AT THE LAKE

Quilt Created By:

Nancy Conrad - Frankfort, Michigan

Anne-Marit Ripe Javiknes - Nordfjordeid, Norway

Solfrid Norvik - Syvde, Norway

Annrid Nerhus - Valldal, Norway

Gerd Villadsen - Molde, Norway

Britt Gjendem Steinstø - Molde, Norway

The Quilt Recipe:

Center: "Snail's Trail" 12" finished block found on page 20.

Triangle Border: "Sawtooth Border" using 2" finished blocks found on page 110.

Appliqué Border: "Hearts Abound Border" found on page 150.

Plain Border: See instructions on "Extension Borders" found on page 9.

Border of Squares: Use the 2 1/4" finished squares (from the four-patch border) found on page 154.

Cut "extension strips" to sew between the squares.

Border of Choice: "Snails Trail Border" found on page 176.

My name is Britt and I live in Molde. I am married to Ole and have two sons and also have a Great Dane. I hope that you will be pleased with your quilt. I am so excited to get my own quilt back. I have been quilting for almost ten years and it occupies my head at all times. I love this hobby.

– Britt Gjendem Steinstø – Molde, Norway

SNAIL'S TRAIL

12" Finished Block

Measurements include 1/4" seam allowance

Cutting Requirements:

    Yellow/Green/Blue/Dot

        Template A: cut 1 in each color

        Template B: cut 1 in each color

        Template D: cut 1 in each color

        Template E: cut 1 in each color

Piecing Guide:

    Sew yellow C to Dot C. Press the seam allowances towards the yellow.

    Sew green C to Blue C. Press the seam allowances towards the blue. Sew these units together.

    Sew the green D to the top of the green/blue squares.

    Sew the dot D to the bottom of the yellow/dot squares.

    Press the seams towards the triangles.

    Sew the yellow D to the green/yellow side.

    Sew the blue D to the blue/dot side.

    Press the seams towards the triangles.

    Sew the yellow B to the yellow/green side.

    Sew the blue B to the dot/blue side.

    Press the seams towards the triangles.

    Sew the Dot B to the yellow/dot side.

    Sew the green B to the green/blue side.

Press the seams towards the triangles.

Sew the yellow A to the yellow/green side.

Sew the blue A to the dot/blue side.

Press the seams towards the triangles.

Sew the dot A to the dot/yellow side.

Sew the green A to the green/blue side.

Press the seams towards the triangles.

Sew the dot E to the dot/yellow side.

Sew the green E to the blue/green side.

Press the seams towards the triangles.

Sew the blue E to the dot/blue sides.

Sew the yellow E to the yellow/green side.

Press the seams towards the triangles.

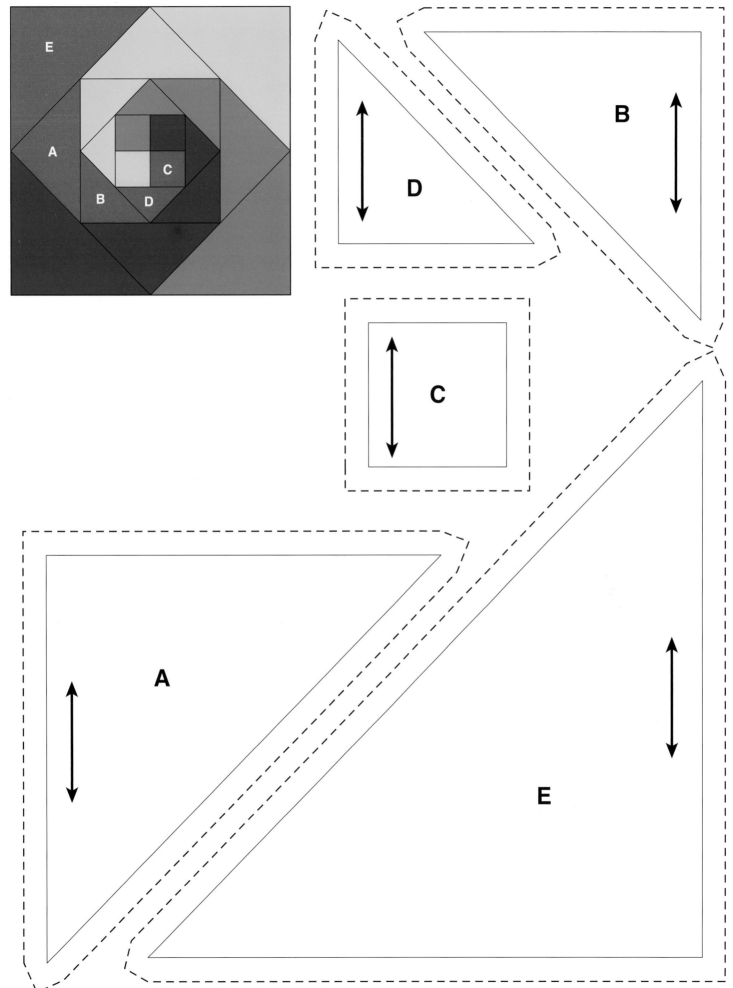

MY FLOWER GARDEN

My Flower Garden

Quilt Created By:

Vera Sandnes - Molde, Norway

Nancy Conrad - Frankfort, Michigan

Paula Kemperman - Belmont, Michigan

Susan Rand - Rockford, Michigan

Jan VanderMolen - Saranac, Michigan

Ardie Sveadas - Sparta, Michigan

The Quilt Recipe:

Center: "Sun Rays" 12" finished block found on page 24.

Triangle Border: "Flying Geese" found on page 99.

Plain Border: See instructions on "Extension Borders" found on page 9.

Appliqué Border: "Signs of Spring Border" found on page 129.

Border of Squares: Plain border is cut 1 1/2"x desired length. These will be sewn on both sides of the border of squares. Use the 1 1/8" finished squares that are found on the four-patch page 154. Sew these together in a single row.

Border of Choice: "Midnight Star" found on page 164.

Plain Border: Cut 2 1/4" x desired length.

I have been quilting since my first son was born in 1962. I have four grown children, the youngest is 24. My nest may be empty but the house is full of quilts! I am very excited about getting to see my block again and the changes made by all of you! An international exchange was a great idea and I am thankful I was chosen to participate. I am so sorry that we could not all meet for coffee and cookies and some good quilting fun. I consider myself a "Transplanted Scandinavian." I hope that you enjoyed it as much. Thank you for all your hard work on my behalf.

– Ardie Sveadas – Sparta, Michigan

SUN RAYS

12" Finished Block

Measurements include 1/4" seam allowance.

Cutting requirements:

Template A: cut 1

Template B: cut 8

Template C: cut 4

Template D: cut 8

Template E: cut 8

Template F: cut 4

Sewing Guide:

Star Points: Sew D to C. Make four units. Press the seam allowance towards D. Sew D to the other side of C. Press seam allowance towards D. Sew B to the side of this unit. Press the seam allowance towards B. Sew B to the other side of the unit. Sew these units to the top and bottom of A. Press seam allowance towards the center.

Corner Squares: Sew two E pieces together. Make four units. Press the seams towards the darker fabric. Sew F to the top of these squares. Press the seam allowance towards F. Sew the corner squares to the ends of two star points. Press the seam allowance towards the corner squares.

Sew to the sides of the star.

  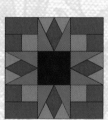

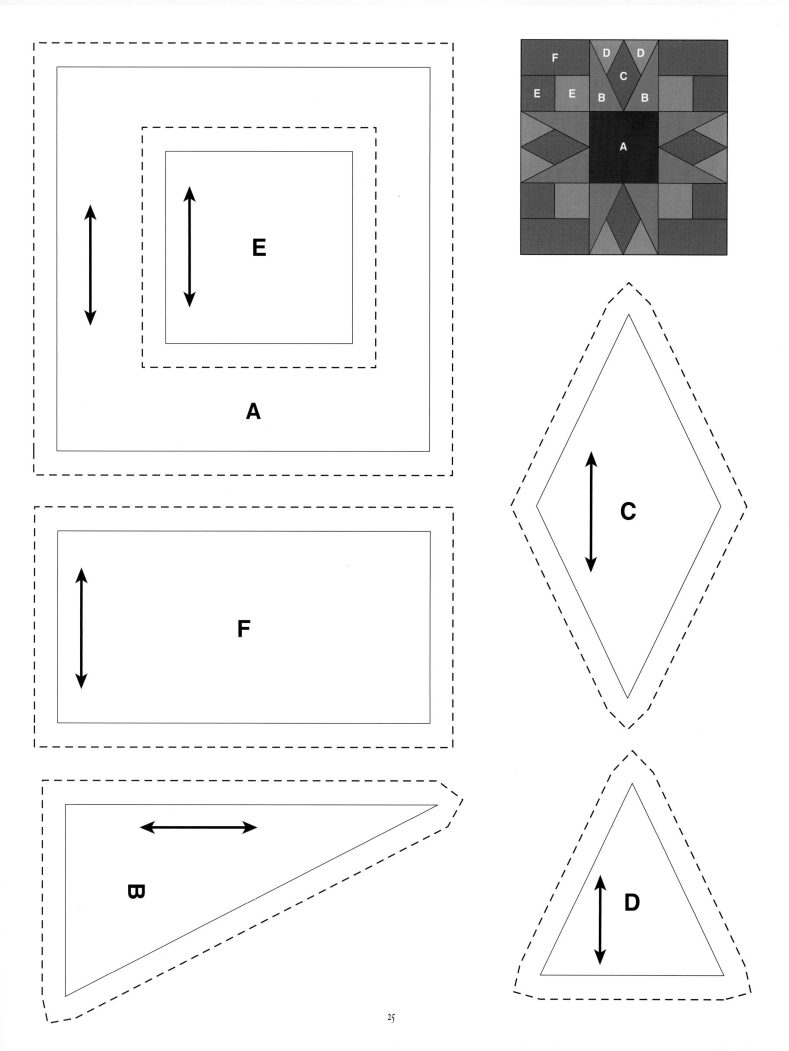

E

A

F

C

B

D

25

DREAM BASKET

DREAM BASKET

Quilt Created By:

Marjorie Nelson - Frankfort, Michigan

Susie Vigland - Benzonia, Michigan

Emilie Kimpel - Arcadia, Michigan

Rebecca Nelson-Zerfas - Beulah, Michigan

Cindy Larson - Frankfort, Michigan

Marjorie Nelson - Frankfort, Michigan

Machine Quilted By: Deborah J. Yezbak - Traverse City, Michigan

The Quilt Recipe:

Center: "Dream Flowers" 6" x 12" finished rectangle found on page 28.

Triangle Border: "Square Pathway" found on page 108.

Appliqué Border: "Floral Garland" found on page 135.

Plain Border: See instructions on "Extension Borders" page 9.

Border of Squares: Made of a combination of 4" finished "Hourglass" blocks found on page 97 and 2" finished "Sawtooth" blocks sewn together to make pinwheel blocks. Directions found on page 110.

Plain Border: Cut the first border 1 1/4" x desired length. Cut the next border 2 1/4" x the desired length.

My name is Susie Vigland from Benzonia, Michigan. I am the first to work on your block. We were told to try something new and use triangles. Well I used triangles which I have never done before and I learned a lot!

– Susie Vigland – Benzonia, Michigan

DREAM FLOWERS

Designed by: Marjorie Nelson - Frankfort, Michigan

Finished Size: 6" x 12" Rectangle

Use your favorite appliqué technique and add 1/4" seam allowance if you are appliquéing by hand.

Cut background: 6 1/2" x 12 1/2" rectangle.

Basket: Vertical strips: cut 9 -- 3/4" x 6" strips

       Horizontal strips: cut 13 -- 3/4" x 4" strips

       Press under 1/4" on each side of the strip.

The Basket:

Use the basket layout as a guide to weave the basket. Start at the bottom of the basket and alternate weaving under and over until the basket shape is filled. Trim the excess fabric from the sides, top and bottom of the basket. Place the basket on the background. Appliqué the side pieces to the basket and then the top and bottom. The top, bottom and side pieces will hold the basket in place.

Flowers: template C: cut 5 each of two different colors.

       Flower Centers: template F: cut 2

       Leaves: template D: cut 10

       Berries: template E: cut 22

Appliqué the pieces to the background.

Butterfly: cut 1 body template G.

Wings: cut 2 - 2 1/2" squares of fabric. Iron a piece of fusible web to the wrong side of the fabric. Peel away the paper back. Place the second piece of fabric with the wrong side toward the fusible web and iron. From this piece cut out 1 template H and 1 H reversed.

Follow the same instructions for template I.

Place the wings under the body and appliqué to the background .

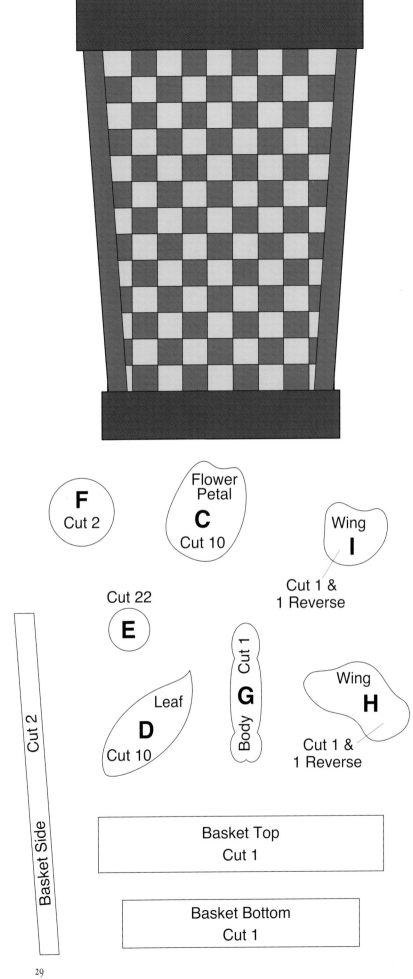

F
Cut 2

Flower
Petal
C
Cut 10

Wing
I
Cut 1 &
1 Reverse

Cut 22
E

Cut 2

Basket Side

Leaf
D
Cut 10

Body G Cut 1

Wing
H
Cut 1 &
1 Reverse

Basket Top
Cut 1

Basket Bottom
Cut 1

LIFE IS LIKE A MERRY-GO-ROUND

LIFE IS LIKE A MERRY-GO-ROUND

Quilt Created By:

Ann Karin Myren - Tennfjord, Norway

Rebecca Nelson-Zerfas - Beulah, Michigan

Linda Hamel - Frankfort, Michigan

Cindy Larson - Frankfort, Michigan

Jo Black Danford - Beulah, Michigan

Emilie Schubert Kimpel - Arcadia, Michigan

The Quilt Recipe:

Center Square: "Seasons of Change" 12" finished block found on page 32.

Triangle Border: "Hourglass Border" using 3 1/2" finished squares. Instructions on page 97.

A 1 1/2" wide plain border was added before the hourglass border.

Plain Border: See instructions on "Extension Borders" found on page 9.

Appliqué Border: "Seasons of Trees Border" found on page 139.

Border of Squares: "Four-Patch Border" using 2" finished squares. Instructions on page 154.

Border of Choice: Plain border cut 4 3/4" x desired length.

As Time Goes By
- Morning, Day, Evening, Night
- Winter, Spring, Summer, Autumn
- Year after year
- New Millennium
Just like a merry-go-round

– Ann Karin Myren – Tennfjord, Norway

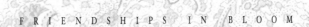

SEASONS OF CHANGE

12" Finished Block

All measurements include 1/4" seam allowance.

Cutting requirements:

Template A: cut one 8" square.

Template B: cut four 2 3/4" x 8" rectangles.

Template C: cut four 2 3/4" squares.

Piecing Guide:

Sew a rectangle to opposite sides of the center square. Press the seam allowance towards the center.

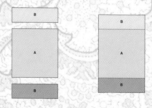

Sew the corner squares to the ends of the other two rectangles. Press the seam allowance towards the squares. Sew these units to the other sides of the center square.

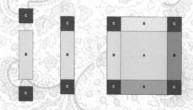

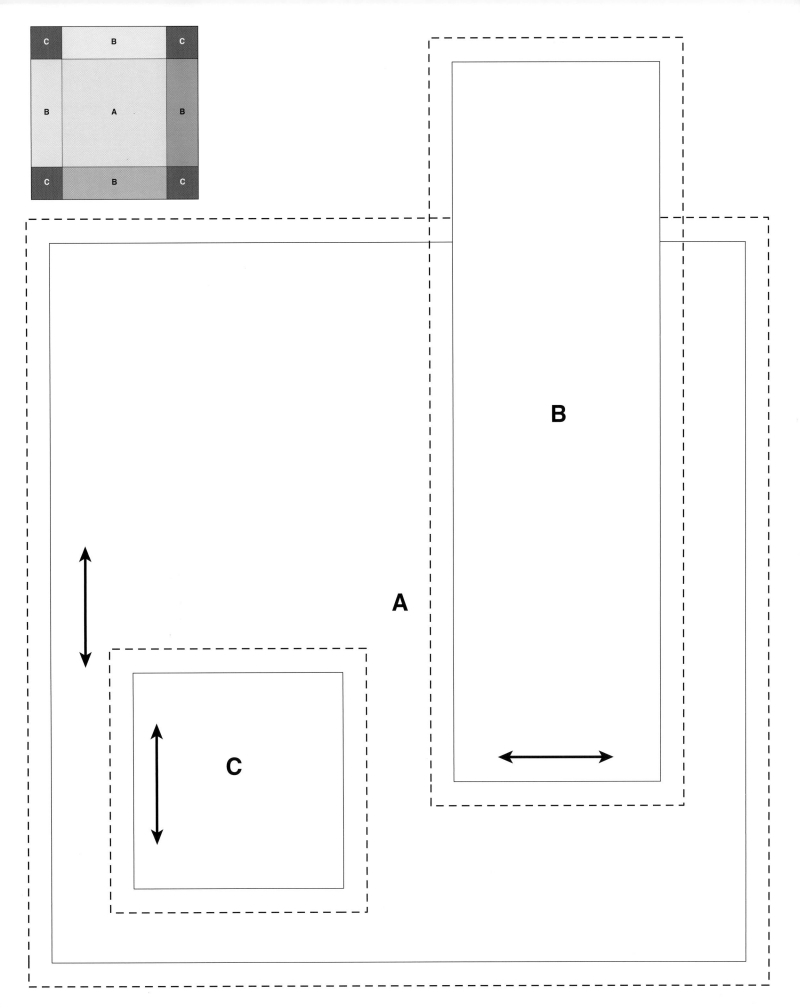

POLAR NIGHT

POLAR NIGHT

Quilt Created By:

Mariann Hatlenes - Stårheim, Norway

Susie Vigland - Benzonia, Michigan

Lois Lewis - Boyne City, Michigan

Marjorie Nelson - Frankfort, Michigan

Rebecca Nelson-Zerfas - Beulah, Michigan

Emilie Kimpel - Arcadia, Michigan

The Quilt Recipe:

Center: "Polar Star" 12 1/2" finished block found on page 36.

Triangle Border: "Shark's Tooth" finished 2 1/2" found on page 104.

Plain Border: "Fence Border" found on page 118.

Appliqué Border: "Starry Path" found on page 143.

Plain Border: See instructions on "Extension Borders" found on page 9.

Border of Squares: "Irish Chain Border" found on page 159.

Border of Choice: "Prairie Points Border" found on page 178.

My home is in Nordfjord, a small place on the west coast near the North Sea. Stårheim is a small village (500 people) in one of our famous fjords, with beautiful nature and fantastic glaciers and mountains. I am married to Olav and we have four children. I live on a small farm with a lot of romantic animals: cat, horse, rabbits and hen.

– Mariann Hatlenes – Stårheim, Norway

POLAR STAR BLOCK

Finished Size 12 1/2" square

Paper Pieced Star:

Cut the pieces for the paper pieced star at least 3/4" larger than the pieces. This will allow for more wiggle room when paper piecing the star. Do this <u>only</u> for the star block and <u>not the log cabin pieces.</u>

Paper Piecing Instructions:

Think of paper piecing as sewing by number.

You will need to sew on the printed side so that the sewing line is facing you. Sew on the solid lines. It's easier to tear the paper off at the end if you use small stitches.

1. With your fingers, make a crease in the paper along the sewing line between #1 and #2. Turn the paper over so the blank side is facing you. Feel for the crease you made. Place the first fabric right side up. Place the next piece of fabric with the right side facing the first fabric. (The back of fabric #2 should be towards you.) While holding the fabric in place, turn the paper over. The printed side should be facing you and the fabrics should be underneath the paper. Sew on the solid line. Trim the seam allowance to 1/4." Press the fabric so you have both right sides facing you. Make a crease where the next sewing line is. Place the next fabric so the wrong side is facing you. Turn it over and sew on the solid line. Make sure you trim the seam allowance and press as you go. Sew on piece 3 in the same manner.

2. After you are finished, trim the seams and leave 1/4" seam allowance along the outside edge. Sew the three sections together. Carefully tear the paper off the back.

Log Cabin:

Cut the following: Includes 1/4" seam allowance.

    Strip A: cut 1 3/4" x 5 1/2"
    Strip B: cut 1 3/4" x 6 3/4"
    Strip C: cut 1 3/4" x 6 3/4"
    Strip D: cut 1 3/4" x 8"
    Strip E: cut 1 3/4" x 8"
    Strip F: cut 1 3/4" x 9 1/4"
    Strip G: cut 1 3/4" x 9 1/4"
    Strip H: cut 1 3/4" x 10 1/2"
    Strip I: cut 1 1/2" x 10 1/2"
    Strip J: cut 1 1/2" x 11 1/2"
    Strip K: cut 1 1/2" x 11 1/2"
    Strip L: cut 1 1/2" x 12 1/2"

Sew the logs around the star starting with strip A and end with strip L. Press the seam allowances towards the outside of the block after each log is sewn on.

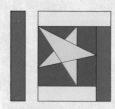

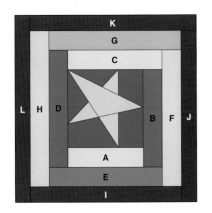

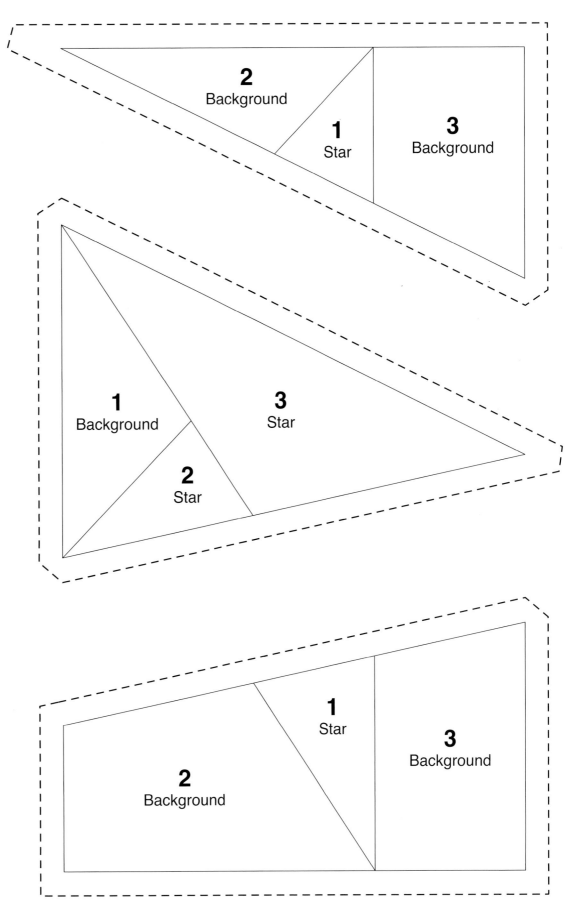

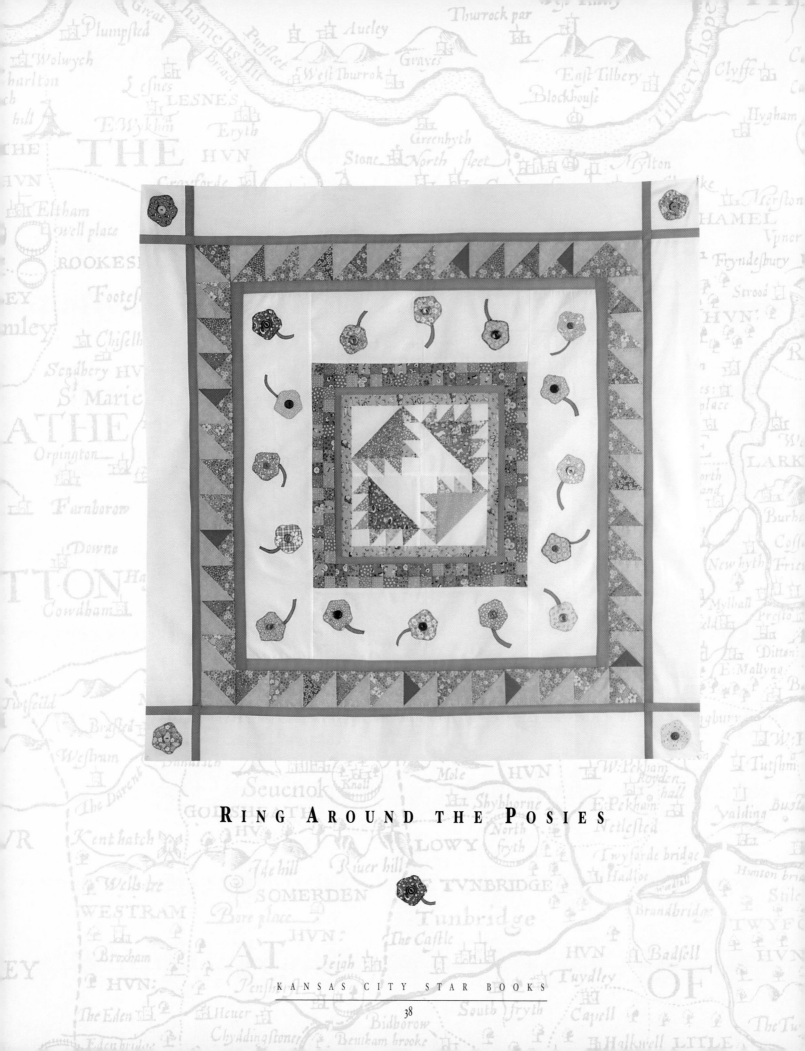

RING AROUND THE POSIES

RING AROUND THE POSIES

Quilt Created By:

Nancy Conrad - Frankfort, Michigan

Marjorie Nelson - Frankfort, Michigan

Nancy Conrad - Frankfort, Michigan

Rebecca Nelson-Zerfas - Beulah, Michigan

Linda Hamel - Frankfort, Michigan

The Quilt Recipe:

Center: "Lawyer's Puzzle" 12" finished block found on page 40.

Plain Border: See instructions "Extension Borders" found on page 9.

Border of Squares: "Four-Patch" using 1" finished squares found on page 154.

Appliqué Border: "Button Flower" found on page 142.

Plain Border: See instructions on "Extension Border" found on page 9.

Triangle Border: "Split Hourglass" using 3" finished block. Pattern found on page 97.

Border of Choice: Plain border with "Button Flowers" in the corners. Cut background 4 1/2" x desired length.

My name is Nancy Conrad and I live in Frankfort, Michigan with my husband Richard. We have three grown children. I just completed my center square. I used a traditional design out of the 1930 reproduction fabrics.

– Nancy Conrad – Frankfort, Michigan

LAWYER'S PUZZLE

12" Finished Block

Measurements include 1/4" seam allowance.

Cutting requirements:

Background Fabric: Template A: cut 4

Template B: cut 24

Template C: cut 4

Assorted Colors: Template B: cut 24

Template A: cut 4

Piecing Guide:

Sew background B to color B. Make 24 units. Press the seam allowances towards the colored fabric. Sew together eight units of 3. Press the seam allowances all to the same side.

Sew background A to color A. Make 4 units. Press the seam allowance towards the colored fabric.

Sew the small triangle units to one side of the large triangle units. Press the seam allowance towards the large triangle unit.

Sew the background squares to the end of the remaining small triangle units. Press the seam allowance towards the corner squares. Sew to the other side of the large triangle unit.

 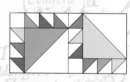

Sew the blocks together as shown.

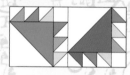

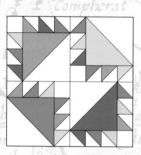

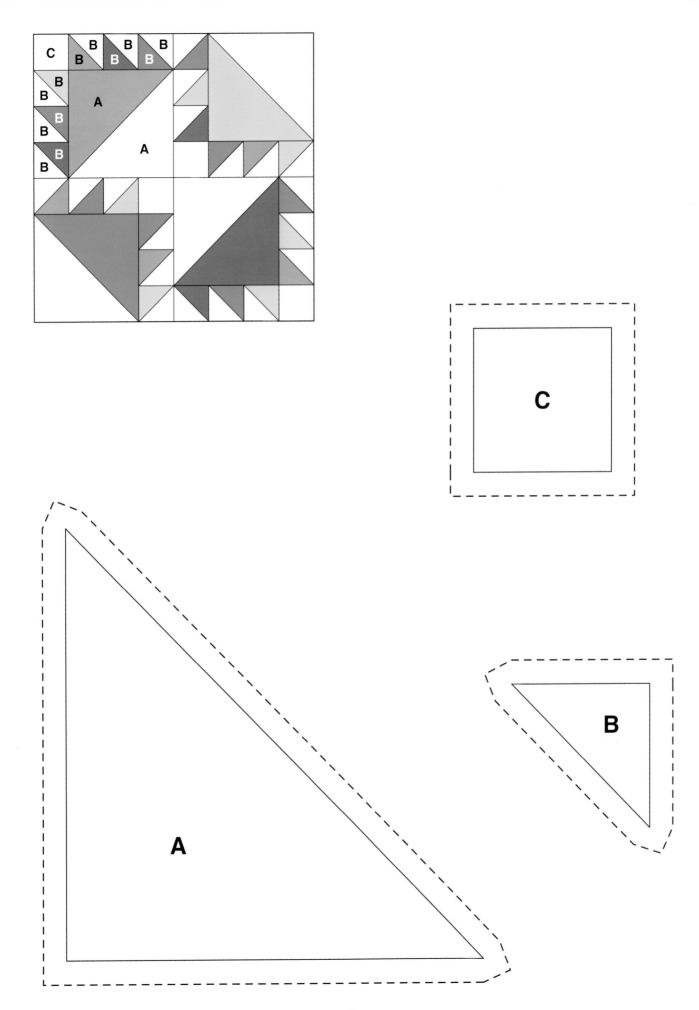

PANSIES

PANSIES

Quilt Created By:

Rebecca Nelson-Zerfas - Beulah, Michigan

Cindy Larson - Frankfort, Michigan

Marjorie Nelson - Frankfort, Michigan

Emilie Kimpel - Arcadia, Michigan

Rebecca Nelson-Zerfas - Beulah, Michigan

The Quilt Recipe:

Center Square: "Pansy Center" 6" x 12" finished block found on page 44.

Triangle Border: "Sawtooth Border" with 1" finished squares found on page 110.

Appliqué Border: "Celtic Cables" found on page 144.

Plain Border: See directions on "Extension Borders" found on page 9.

Border of Squares: "Nine-Patch" using 3/4" finished squares found on page 154.

Make alternating solid squares cut 2 3/4".

Border of Choice: Border is cut 4" wide by desired length.

My center block was inspired by the pansies that grow in my flower boxes. They are about the only things besides weeds that I can get to grow. I am anxiously waiting to see what each one of you will add to this.

– Rebecca Nelson-Zerfas - Beulah, Michigan

PANSY CENTER

Designed By: Rebecca Nelson-Zerfas, Beulah, Michigan

Finished block: 6" x 12"

Use your favorite appliqué technique and add 1/4" seam allowance if appliquéing by hand.

Background: cut a 6 1/2" x 12 1/2" rectangle.

Pansies: from gold fabric, cut 1 each of templates A,B,C,D.

From purple fabric, cut 1 each of templates E-T.

Buds: cut 1 each of templates U,V,W,X,Y,Z.

From leaf and stem fabric, cut 1 each of the following templates 1-21.

Grass: cut 1 each of the grass templates.

Appliqué all to the background.

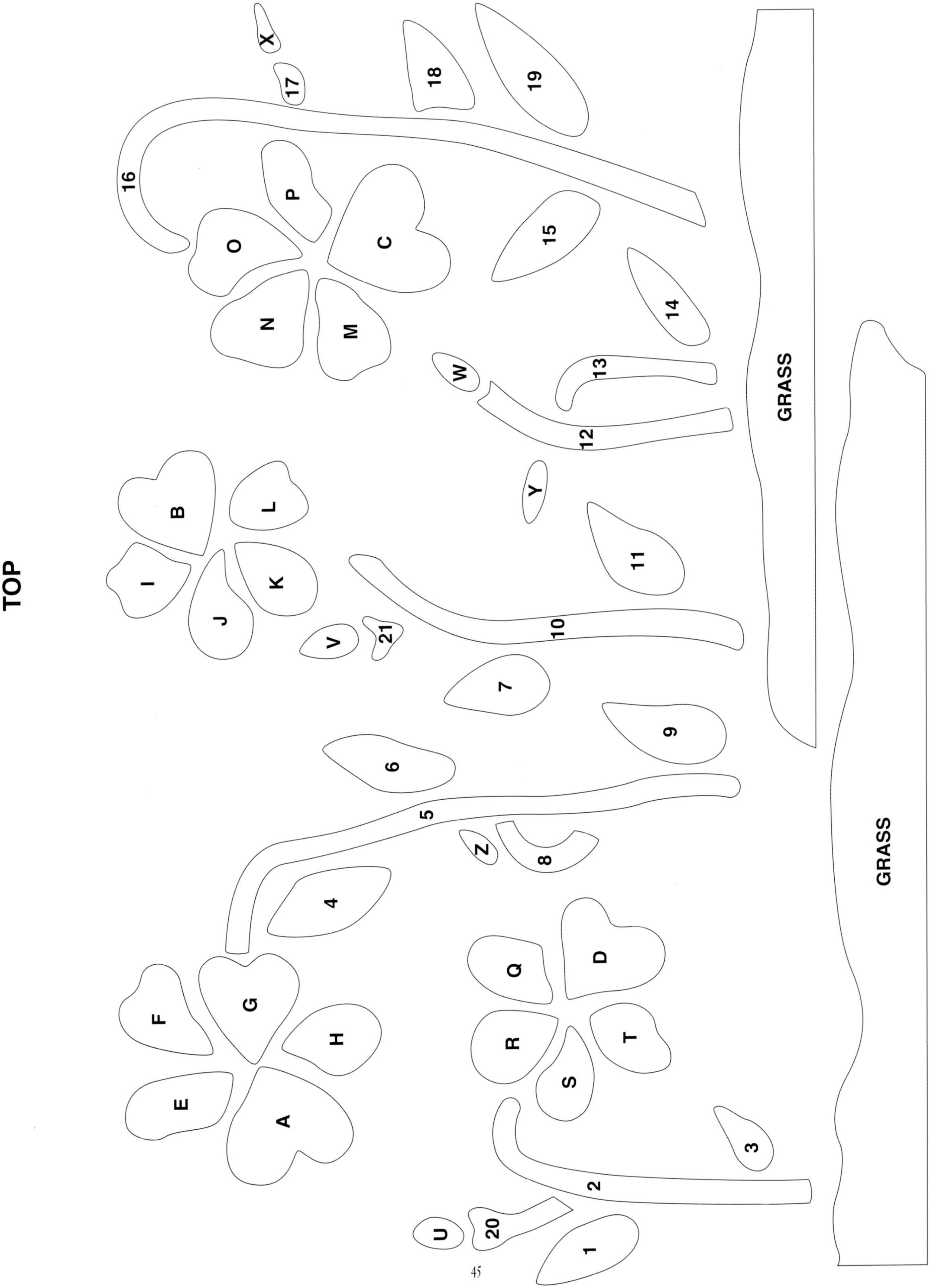

TOP

X

17

18

19

16

P

O

C

N

M

15

14

W

13

12

Y

B

I

L

J

K

V

21

11

10

7

9

6

5

Z

8

4

F

G

E

H

A

Q

D

R

S

T

3

2

U

20

1

GRASS

GRASS

45

SERENITY

SERENITY

Quilt Created By:

Jo Black Danford - Beulah, Michigan

Karin Bjerke - Molde, Norway

Anne Grete Nakken - Molde, Norway

Gerd Villadsen - Molde, Norway

Kristine Rønning - Sekken, Norway

Annrid Nerhus - Valldal, Norway

The Quilt Recipe

Center Square: 12" finished "Serenity" block found on page 48.

Triangle Border: New York Beauty Border found on page 106.

Appliqué Border: Cherry Blossom Border found on page 137.

Plain Border: See directions on extension borders on page 9.

Border of squares: 2" finished "Four-Patch" border on page 154.

Border of choice: This is a plain border cut 5 1/2" x desired length. Cut four 5 1/2" corner squares.

These words come from Molde, Norway. I must say I was immediately attracted by your block—among the many beauties from your quilting friends in Michigan. It has been nice to work with the block, but it took me some time to find out how to continue. I didn't want to take away the focus from your block. I chose to frame it with some darker colors in addition to a repetition of the circles in the triangle blocks. .

— Karin Bjerke – Molde, Norway

SERENITY CENTER

Finished Size 12 1/2" square

Measurements include 1/4" seam allowance.

Cutting requirements:

Template A: cut 9 from assorted fabrics.

Template B: cut 3

Template C: cut 6

Template D: cut 3

Piecing guide: Sew piece A to C. Make six units. Press seams towards A.

Sew piece B to D. Then sew this unit to A. Make three units.

Sew together three rows of three. Then sew the rows together.

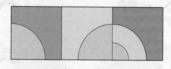
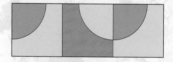

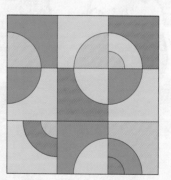

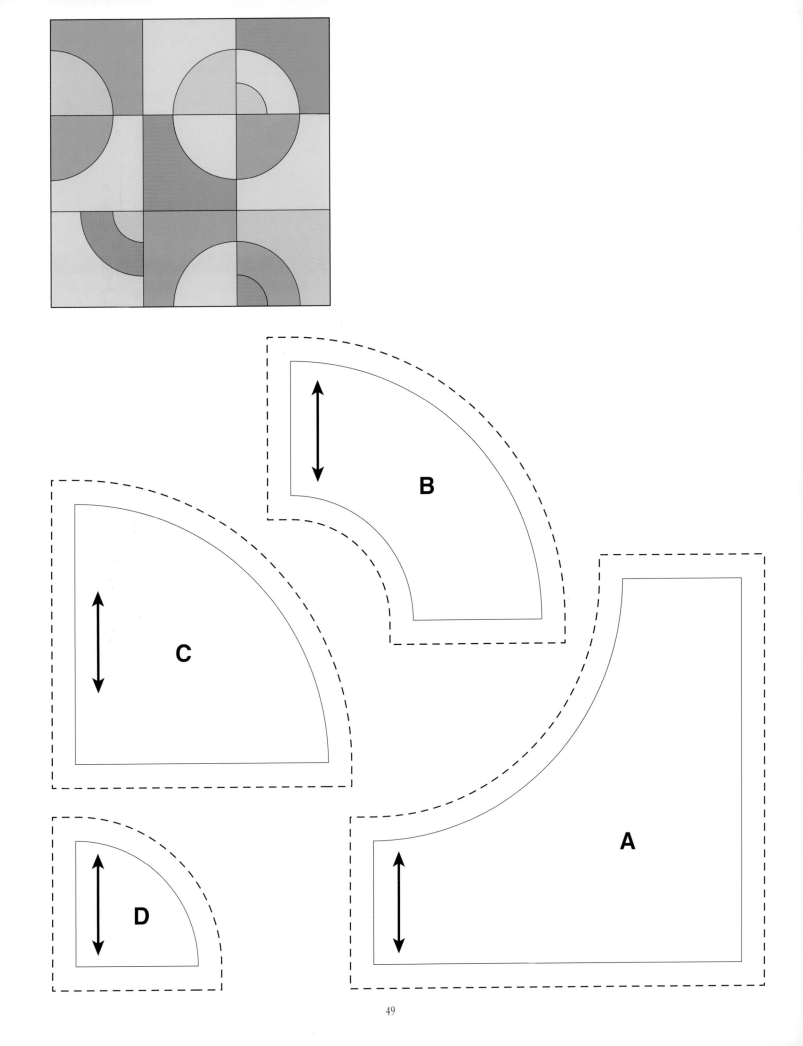

B

C

D

A

BELL FLOWER LOCALLY GROWN

BELL FLOWER LOCALLY GROWN

Quilt Created By:

Ardie Sveadas - Sparta, Michigan

Jackie Huizen - Hudsonville, Michigan

Paula Kemperman - Belmont, Michigan

Marjorie Nelson - Frankfort, Michigan

Rebecca Nelson-Zerfas - Beulah, Michigan

Ardie Sveadas - Sparta, Michigan

The Quilt Recipe:

Center: "Bell Flower" 6" finished square found on page 52.

Triangle Border: "Split Hourglass" 2" finished blocks found on page 97.

Appliqué Border: "Dragonflies in Flight" found on page 123.

Plain Border: See instructions on "Extension Border" found on page 9.

Border of Squares: "Four-Patch" with 3/4" finished squares found on page 154.

Border of Choice: "Curvy Path" found on page 167.

Hello, My name is Ardie Sveadas. I live in Sparta, Michigan. It's a rural farming area known for growing apples. Quilting has a way of keeping you once it has taken you in. I still love the creativeness and colors, as well as the feel of fabric in my fingers. I like all aspects of the medium from the piecing to the binding. Best of all applique!!! May all your seams be a quarter inch.

– Ardie Sveadas – Sparta, Michigan

BELL FLOWER

Designed by: Ardie Sveadas - Sparta, Michigan

6" Finished Block

Use your favorite appliqué technique and add 1/4" seam allowance if you are appliquéing by hand.

Background Fabric: cut 1 - 6 1/2" square.

Flowers: cut 1 each of template A and B.

cut 1 each of templates C and D.

cut 1 each templates E and F (Green).

Berries: cut 8 pieces using template G.

Leaves and Stems: cut 1 of each piece templates H-Z.
Use various shades of green. Use the placement guide for layout.

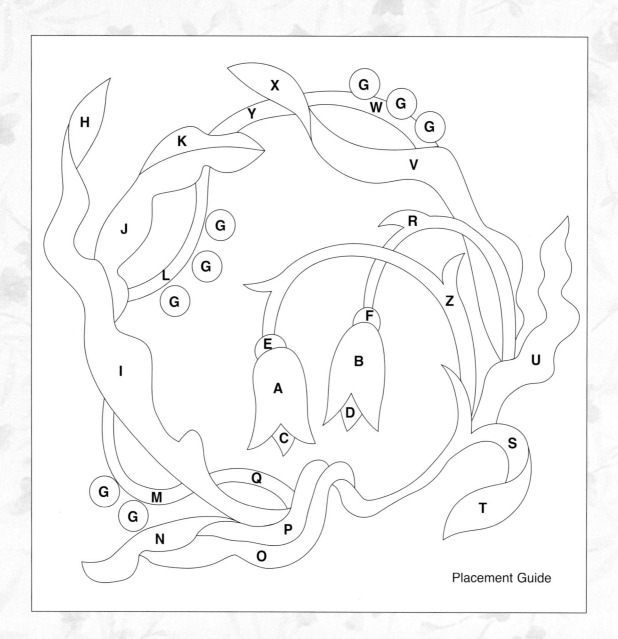

Placement Guide

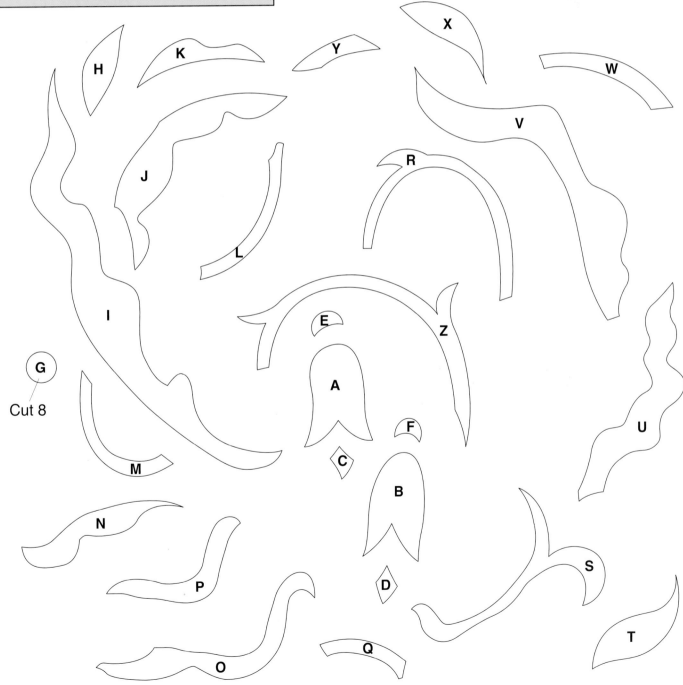

H

K

Y

X

W

V

R

J

L

I

E

Z

G

Cut 8

A

U

M

F

C

B

N

S

P

D

O

Q

T

WINTER SOLSTICE

WINTER SOLSTICE

Quilt Created By:

Rebecca Nelson-Zerfas - Beulah, Michigan

Ardie Sveadas - Sparta, Michigan

Jackie Huizen - Hudsonville, Michigan

Paula Kemperman - Belmont, Michigan

Marjorie Nelson - Frankfort, Michigan

Rebecca Nelson-Zerfas - Beulah, Michigan

The Quilt Recipe:

Center Square: "Holly Leaf" 6" finished block found on page 56.

Triangle Border: "Shark's Tooth Border" 1 1/2" finished found on page 104.

Appliqué Border: "Holly Berry Border" found on page 127.

Plain Border: See instructions on "Extension Borders" found on page 9.

Border of Squares: "Log Cabin Squares" finished 2 1/2" found on page 157.

Border of Choice: Narrow plain border cut 7/8" x desired length. Cut four 7/8" corner squares.

The outside border is cut 2 1/4" x the desired length.

This round robin has brought about such an exchange of ideas and creativeness. We certainly have shared and learned from each other.

– Mom (Marjorie Nelson) – Frankfort, Michigan

HOLLY LEAF

Designed by: Rebecca Nelson-Zerfas - Beulah, Michigan

6" Finished Block

Use your favorite appliqué technique. Add 1/4" seam allowance if
you are hand appliquéing.

Background: cut a 6 1/2" square.

Holly Leaves: cut 4.

Berries: cut 3.

Appliqué to background.

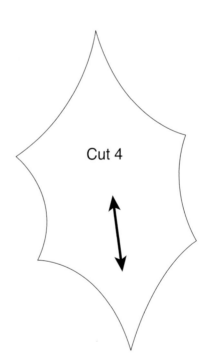

Cut 4

Cut
3

REBECCA'S FLOWERS

REBECCA'S FLOWERS

Quilt Created By:

Rebecca Nelson-Zerfas - Beulah, Michigan

Linda Hamel - Frankfort, Michigan

Rebecca Nelson-Zerfas - Beulah, Michigan

Marjorie Nelson - Frankfort, Michigan

Nancy Conrad - Frankfort, Michigan

The Quilt Recipe:

Center: "Circle of Flowers" 12" finished block found on page 60.

Triangle Border: "Butterflies in Flight" found on page 112.

Appliqué: "Flower Path" found on page 145.

Border of Squares: "Square in Square" 3" finished blocks found on page 161.

Border of Choice: Plain border cut 3 1/2" x desired length.

I am so pleased to be able to share this experience with my quilting friends. It will be a challenge to create unique borders for such special people. As you all know, I consider myself to be Appliqué challenged. Therefore I created somewhat square flowers that can easily be appliquéd. With practice I hope to someday be able to appliqué something other than square flowers!

– Rebecca Nelson-Zerfas – Beulah, Michigan

CIRCLE OF FLOWERS

Designed by: Rebecca Nelson-Zerfas - Beulah, Michigan

10" Finished Block

Use your favorite method of appliqué and add a 1/4" seam allowance if you are appliquéing by hand.

Cutting Guide:

Background: cut 1 - 10 1/2" square.

Flowers: cut 4 blue

cut 4 pink

Flower Center: cut 4 yellow

Leaves: cut 8 green

Vine: cut 4 green

Appliqué the pieces to the background. Sew the pink flowers on top of the blue flowers. See the diagram for placement purposes.

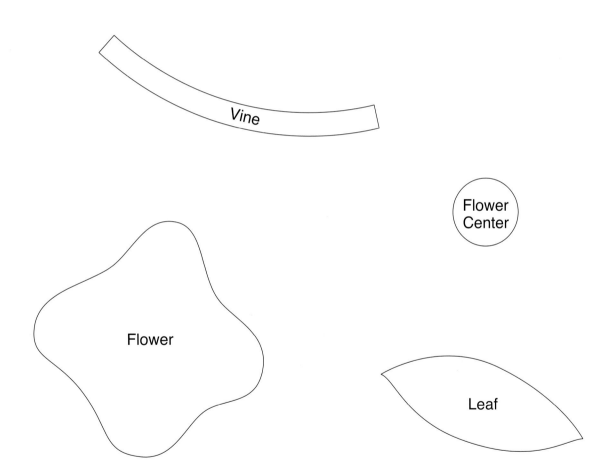

Vine

Flower Center

Flower

Leaf

BASKET OF MEMORIES

BASKET OF MEMORIES

Quilt Created By:

Marjorie Nelson - Frankfort, Michigan

Rebecca Nelson-Zerfas - Beulah, Michigan

Marjorie Nelson - Frankfort, Michigan

Linda Hamel - Frankfort, Michigan

Nancy Conrad - Frankfort, Michigan

Machine Quilted By: Deborah J. Yezbak - Traverse City, Michigan

The Quilt Recipe:

Center: "Memory Basket" 13 1/2" finished block found on page 64.

Triangle Border: Cut two 15" squares and cut in half once on the diagonal. Sew to the hanging.

Make 1" finished sawtooth blocks found on page 110.

Appliqué Border: "Norwegian Rosemale" found on page 121.

Plain Border: See "Extension Borders" found on page 9.

Border of Squares: "Log Cabin" 3 3/4" finished block found on page 157.

Border of Choice: Plain border cut 2" x desired length.

I chose to put your basket on point. I know that you like a lot of quilting and this will give you plenty of room for it! It was a challenge for me to work with only two colors. Your block has a nice crispness to it. I hope that you will like it when it's finished. I look forward to seeing the quilts!   *Your daughter, Rebecca*

– Rebecca Nelson-Zerfas – Beulah, Michigan

MEMORY BASKET

Finished size 13 1/2" square

Measurements include 1/4" seam allowance.

Cutting requirements:

Template A: cut one

Template B: cut one

Template C: cut six light and ten dark

Template D: cut one

Template Dr: cut one

Template E: cut one

Template F: cut one

Basket Handle: cut one 1" x 17 1/2" bias strip

Bow: cut one

Piecing Guide:

Appliqué the handle to piece A. (Turn under 1/4" seam on the handle.)

Sew together the light and dark Cs as shown. Press the seam allowance towards the darker fabric.

Sew the units together as shown. Press the seam allowances all in one direction.

Sew one unit to the side of B. Press seams towards B. Sew piece F to the end of the other unit. Press the seam towards F. Sew this unit to the other side of the basket. Press the seams towards the basket.

Sew piece D to piece C. Sew to side of basket.

Sew piece E to the bottom of the basket. Press the seams towards E.

Sew the basket handle triangle to the top of the basket.

Appliqué the bow to the handle.

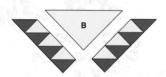 

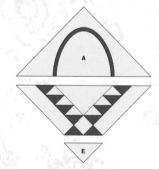 

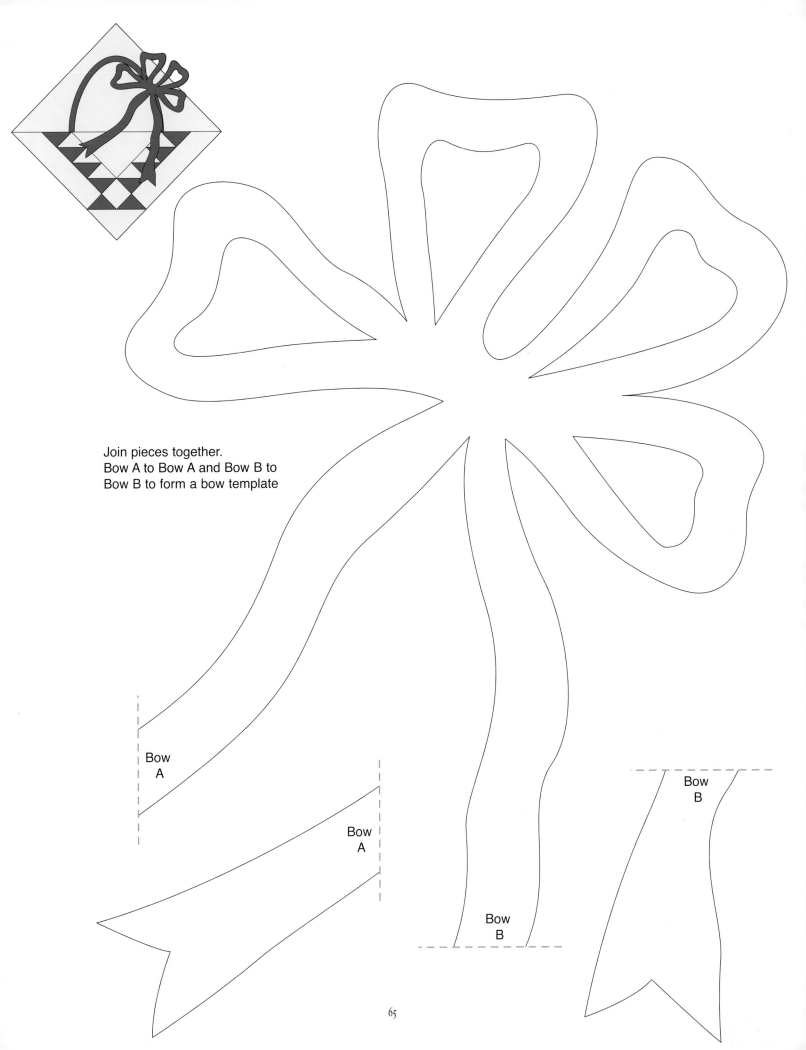

Join pieces together.
Bow A to Bow A and Bow B to
Bow B to form a bow template

Bow
A

Bow
A

Bow
B

Bow
B

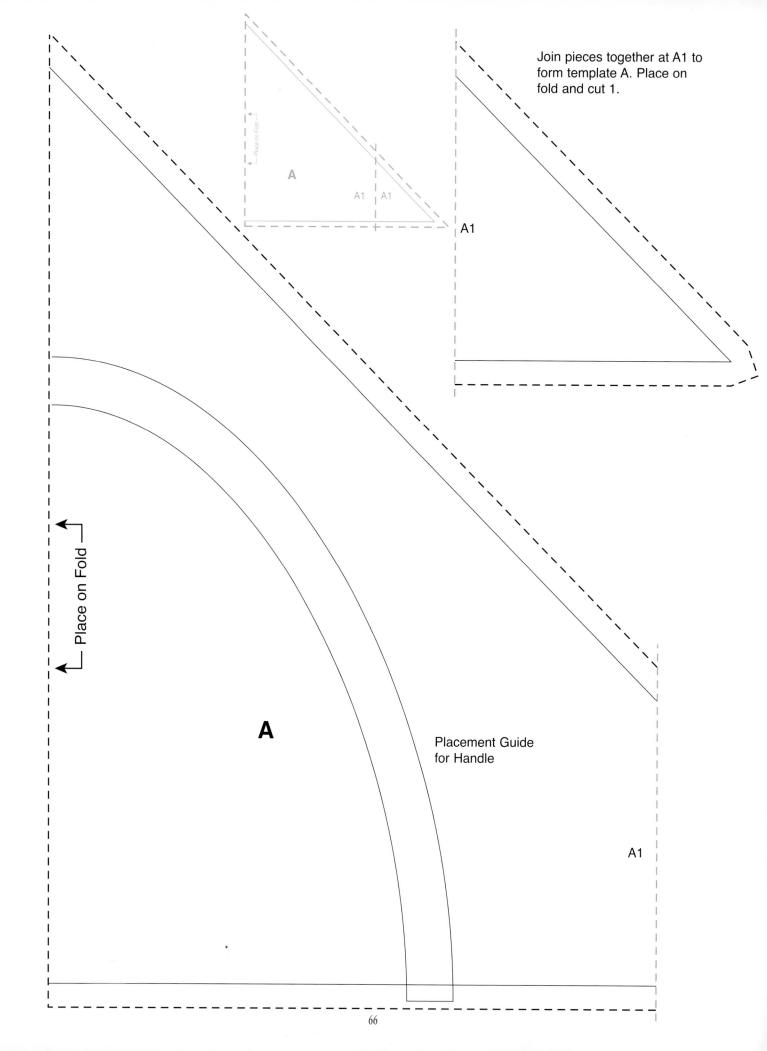

Join pieces together at A1 to form template A. Place on fold and cut 1.

A1

Place on Fold

A

A1

A1

Place on Fold

A

A1

Placement Guide
for Handle

A1

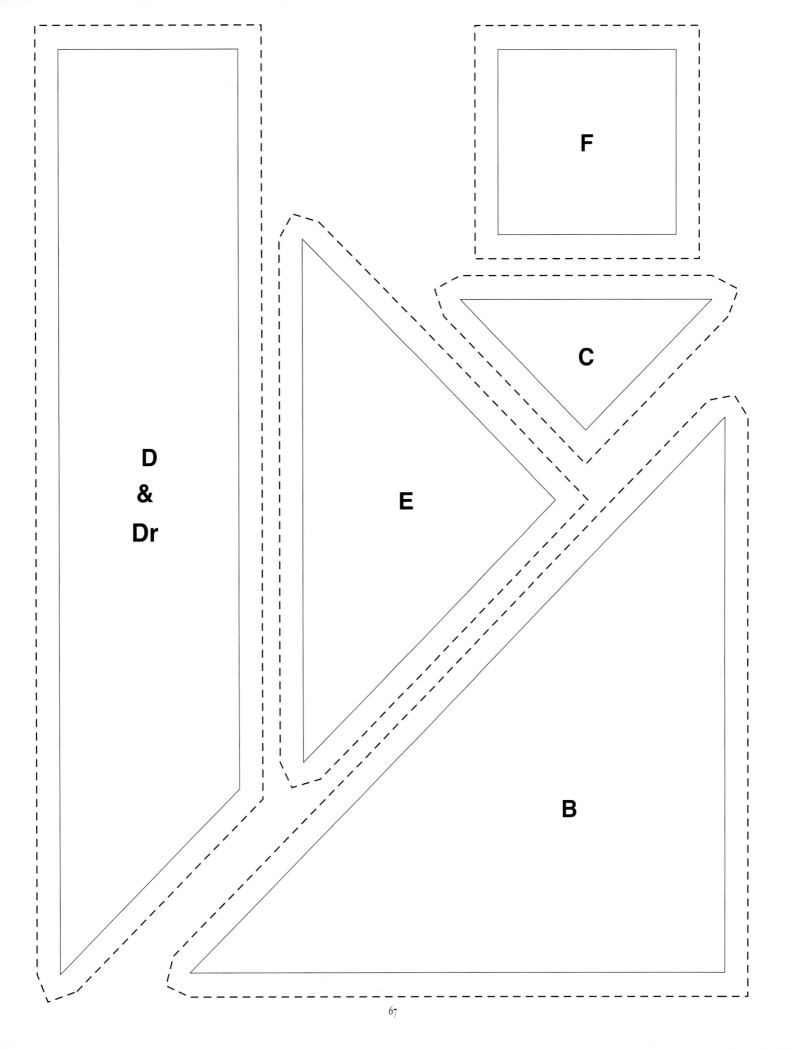

DECEMBER NIGHT

DECEMBER NIGHT

Quilt Created By:

Gerd Villadsen - Molde, Norway

Marjorie Nelson - Frankfort, Michigan

Emilie Kimpel - Arcadia, Michigan

Jo Black Danford - Beulah, Michigan

Rebecca Nelson-Zerfas - Beulah, Michigan

Jackie Huizen - Hudsonville, Michigan

The Quilt Recipe:

Center: "December Star" 12" finished block found on page 70.

Triangle Border: "Sharks Tooth Border" finished 1 3/4" found on page 104.

Plain Border: See instructions on "Extension Borders" found on page 9.

Appliqué Border: "Starry Path Variation" found on page 133.

Border of Squares: "Nine-Patch" using 1" finished squares found on page 154.

Border of Choice: Plain Border cut 1" x desired length. Plain Border cut 4" x desired length.

My name is Gerd, I am married to Kjell and have a son and daughter. Thirteen years ago I started my own quilt shop in Molde. It is fun but a lot of work. I was in Michigan last May visiting Marjorie and Norman Nelson. That area is beautiful. It was so much fun visiting them. There were new experiences every day! Buffalos, Amish families, Gwen Frostics place, garage sales, Sleeping Bear Sand Dunes. I have to go back!!!.

– Gerd Villadsen – Molde, Norway

DECEMBER STAR BLOCK

Finished Size 12" square

All measurements include 1/4" seam allowance.

Cutting requirements:

Fabric #1: Template A: cut 1

Fabric #2: Template B: cut 4

Template C: cut 4

Fabric #3: Template D: cut 4

Fabric #4: Template E: cut 8

Fabric #5 Background: Template E: cut 12

Template F: cut 8

Piecing Guide:

Sew a B triangle to A. Press the seam allowances towards A.

Sew F triangles to E. Press the seam allowances towards E.

Make four units

Sew C to the above units. Press the seam allowance toward C.

Sew D to the above units. Press the seam allowance towards D.

Sew two of these units to opposite sides of the A/B section. Press towards the center.

Sew a background E to fabric number 4 E. Make four of these units. Press seam allowances towards fabric number 4 E. Sew the background E to a background E. Press seam allowances in the opposite direction from above.

Sew these units to the ends of the other two C/D/E/F units. Press the seam allowance towards the small square unit.

Sew the remaining sections to the hanging.

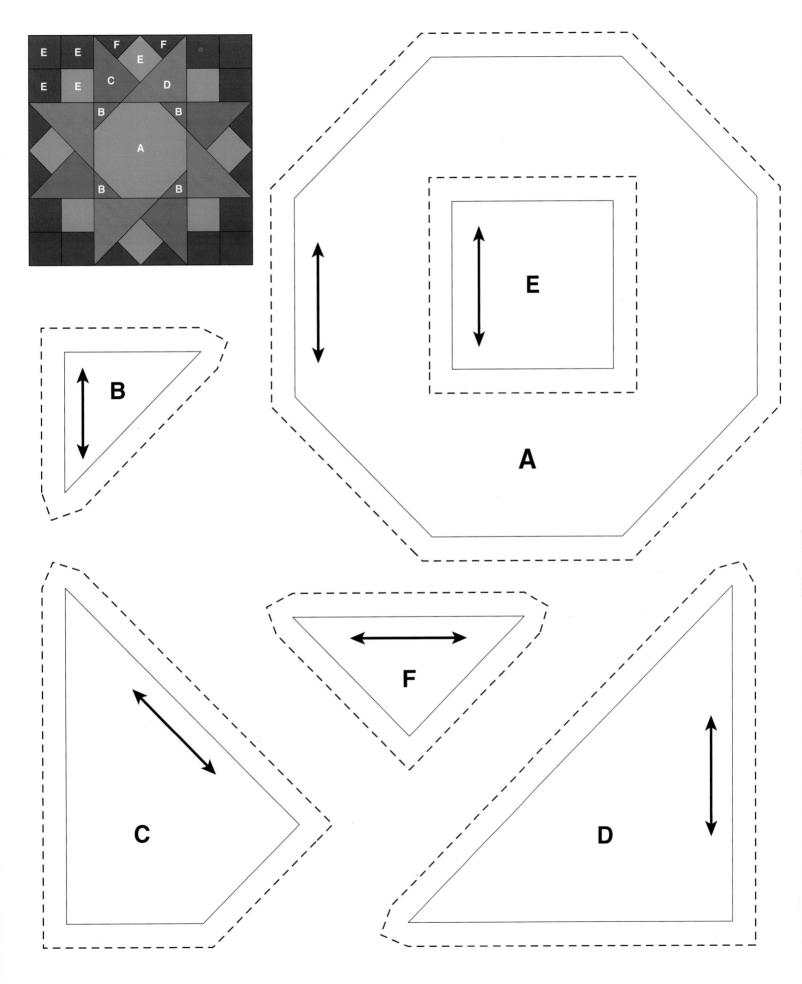

SAMMARBEID ER BARE GLEDE

(WORK TOGETHER IS ALWAYS A JOY)

SAMMARBEID ER BARE GLEDE
(WORK TOGETHER IS ALWAYS A JOY)

Quilt Created By:

Gro Irene Brusdal Helle - Vatne, Norway

Susan Rand - Rockford, Michigan

Jan VanderMolen - Saranac, Michigan

Ardie Sveadas - Sparta, Michigan

Nancy Conrad - Frankfort, Michigan

Paula Kemperman - Belmont, Michigan

The Quilt Recipe

Center Square: "Morning Star Block" 12" finished block found on page 74.

Triangle Border: "On Point Sawtooth" 1 1/2" finished squares found on page 102.

Plain Border: See instructions on "Extension Borders" found on page 9.

Appliqué Border: "Flowers of Norway Border" found on page 146.

Plain Border: See instructions on "Extension Borders" found on page 9.

Border of Squares: "Square in Square Border" using 4" finished blocks found on page 161.

Border of Choice: "Cactus Flower" found on page 183.

I live in a small place named Hellestranda, and the nearest town is Iesund about 60 miles away. In 1988 I married Ole Johan and we have a six-year-old boy, Ole-Petter. I have been sewing since I was a little girl, mostly clothes and curtains. Two years ago I took my first class in patchwork and I was so fascinated. It was so much fun to make something out of different sized pieces and colors of fabrics.

— Gro Irene Helle – Hellestranda, Norway

MORNING STAR BLOCK

12" Finished Block

All measurements include 1/4" seam allowance.

Cutting requirements:

Background: Template A: cut four

Template B: cut four

Star fabric: Template C: star centers cut 8

star middle cut 16

star points cut 8

Piecing guide:

Sew the diamond units together using the C pieces as shown. Press seams towards the dark fabric. Make eight units.

Sew piece B to one of the diamond units. Stop sewing 1/4" from the edges. You may want to press the seam open. Sew a diamond unit to the other side as shown. Press seams open. Make four units like this.

Sew piece A to the unit as shown. Press the seams open.

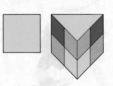 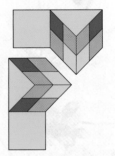

Make four of these units.

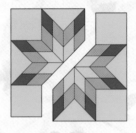 

Sew the units together as shown to complete the block.

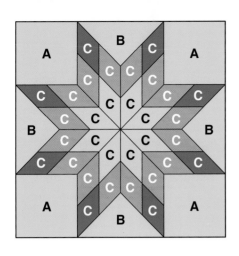

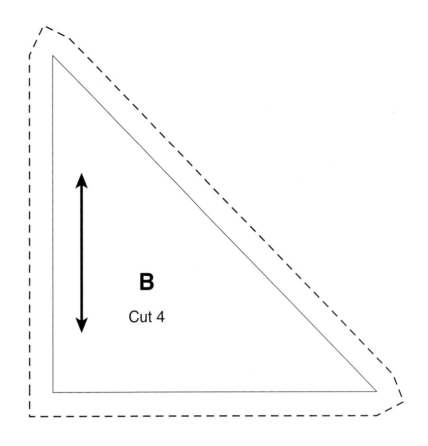

B

Cut 4

C

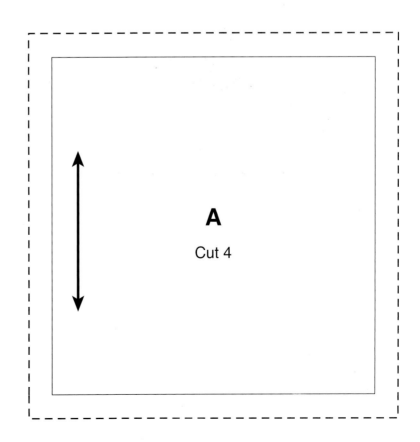

A

Cut 4

BASKET IN THE MIDDLE

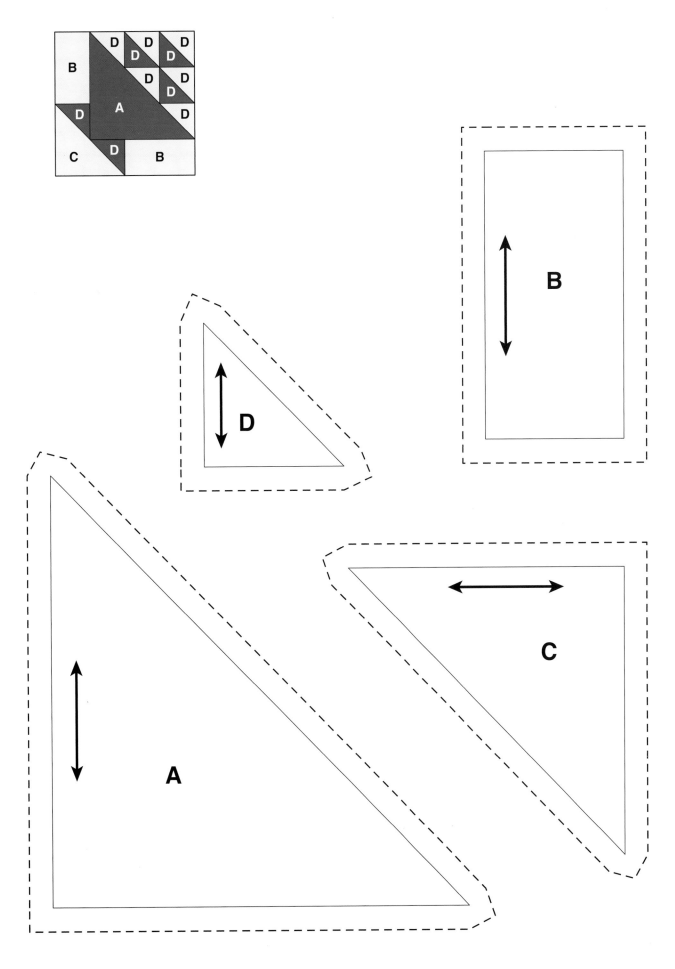

OCEANS OF STARS

OCEANS OF STARS

Quilt Created By:

Marjorie Nelson - Frankfort, Michigan

Annrid Nerhus - Valldal, Norway

Vera Sandnes - Molde, Norway

Gerd Villadsen - Molde, Norway

Eli AF Jensen - Aukra, Norway

Karin Bjerke - Molde, Norway

Machine quilted by: Nancy Roelfsema - Grand Rapids, Michigan

The Quilt Recipe:

Center Square: "Ocean Of Stars" 12" finished block found on page 82.

Triangle Border: "Flying Geese Border" found on page 99.

Appliqué Border: "Stars on Point Border" found on page 149.

Plain Border: "Shooting Stars" found on page 116.

Border of Squares: "Nine-Patch Borders" using 1 1/8" finished squares found on page 154.

Use an alternating 3 7/8" plain block with the nine-patch.

Border of Choice: "Mariners Stars Border" found on page 181.

I have been quilting for about 10-15 years. I love it. Just wish there were some more hours every day. I hope that you will be satisfied with your quilt top when it returns to you.

– Annrid Nerhus – Valldal, Norway

OCEAN OF STARS CENTER BLOCK

Designed by: Marjorie Nelson - Frankfort, Michigan

Finished Block: 12"

Use your favorite appliqué method and add 1/4" seam allowance if appliquéing by hand.

Background: Cut 13" and trim down to 12 1/2" after appliqué is finished.

Appliqués: Template A: place on fold and cut one.

  Template B: cut four

  Template C: cut two

  Template D: cut one

Appliqué piece D in the center of the star. Appliqué the C pieces in the center of D.

The two C pieces are appliquéd one atop the other. The bottom piece is oriented with the points going from east to west and the top piece has the points going north and south.

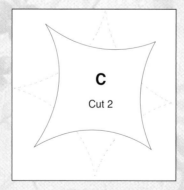

Appliqué the other stars in the corners.

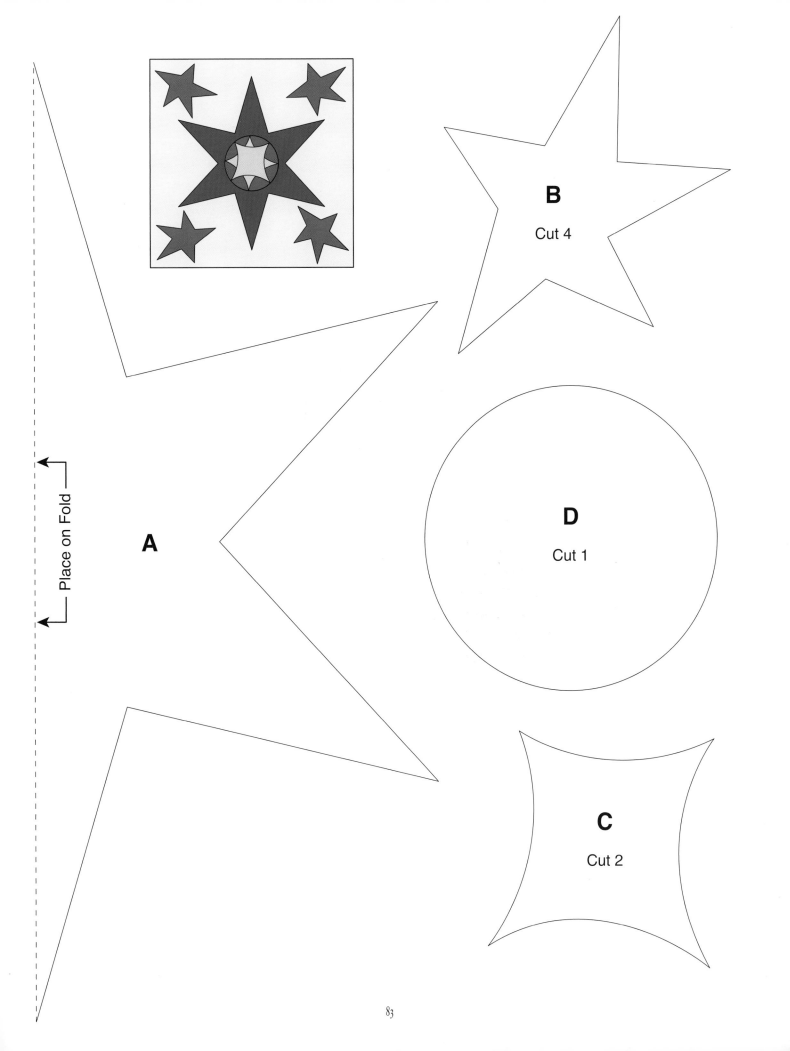

Place on Fold

A

B

Cut 4

D

Cut 1

C

Cut 2

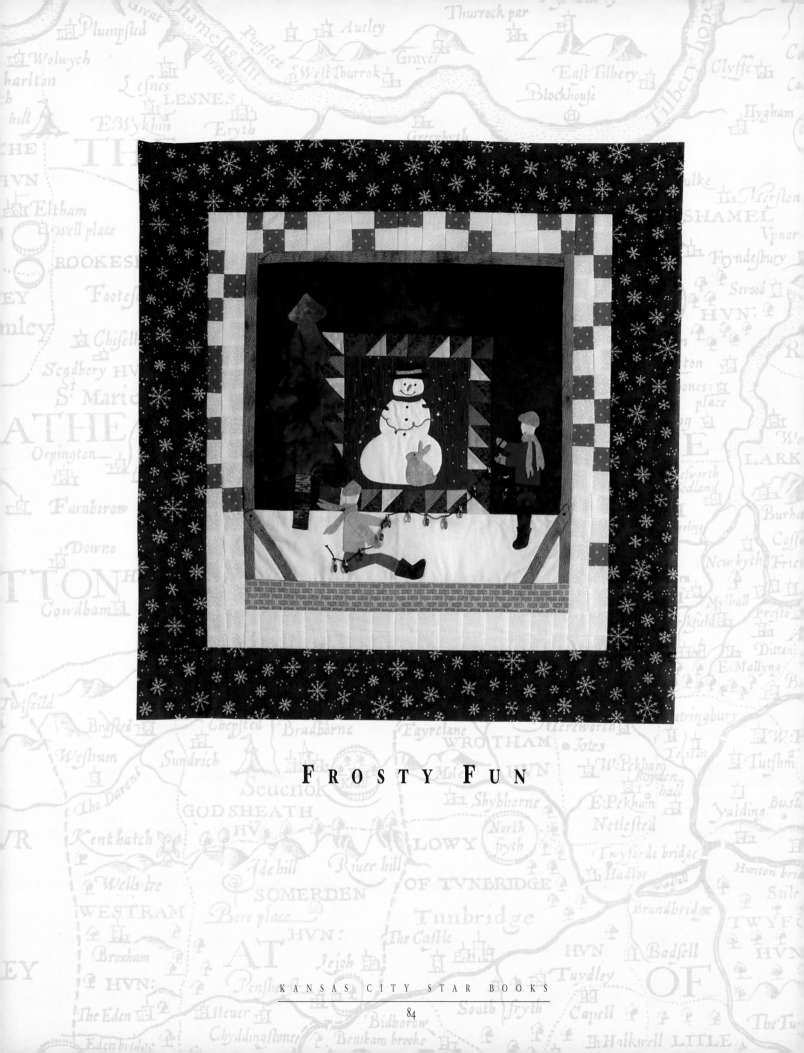

FROSTY FUN

FROSTY FUN

Quilt Created By:

Paula Kemperman - Belmont, Michigan

Marjorie Nelson - Frankfort, Michigan

Rebecca Nelson-Zerfas - Beulah, Michigan

Ardie Sveadas - Sparta, Michigan

Jackie Huizen - Hudsonville, Michigan

Paula Kemperman - Belmont, Michigan

The Quilt Recipe:

Center: "Frosty Fun" 6" finished block found on page 86.

Triangles: "Sawtooth Squares" finished 1". Border found on page 110.

Appliqué: "Trimming The Tree" border found on page 151.

Plain Border: "Framed Border" found on page 117.

Border of Squares: "Winter Path" found on page 156.

Border of Choice: Plain border cut 3 1/2" x desired length.

My name is Paula Kemperman. I live in Belmont, which is a small town near Grand Rapids, Michigan. My husband, Steve and I have two boys, a daughter in-law and a beautiful granddaughter. We like to do many family activities like camping and hiking. We look forward to summer.

– Paula Kemperman – Belmont, Michigan

FROSTY FUN BLOCK

Designed by: Paula Kemperman - Belmont, Michigan

Finished Size: 6" square

Use your favorite appliqué technique and add a 1/4" seam allowance if appliquéing by hand.

Block Background: Cut one 6 1/2" square.

Appliqué the pieces to the background.

Embroider the strand of lights. The light bulbs are embroidered in yellow, white and blue floss. The eyes, mouth, nose and buttons are also embroidered.

Hat Band

Hat

Arm

Scarf

Arm

OUT ON A LIMB

OUT ON A LIMB

Quilt Created By:

Marjorie Nelson - Frankfort, Michigan

Rebecca Nelson-Zerfas - Beulah, Michigan

Ardie Sveadas - Sparta, Michigan

Jackie Huizen - Hudsonville, Michigan

Paula Kemperman - Belmont, Michigan

Marjorie Nelson - Frankfort, Michigan

The Quilt Recipe:

Center: "Out On A Limb" 6" finished block found on page 90.

Triangle Border: "Sawtooth Border" using 1" finished blocks. Instructions found on page 110.

Appliqué Border: "Picture Frame" found on page 148.

Plain Border: See instructions on "Extension Borders" found on page 9.

Border of Squares: "Four-Patch" using 1" finished squares found on page 154.

Plain Border: See instructions on "Extension Borders" found on page 9.

Border of Choice: "Log Cabin Border" using 2 1/2" finished blocks found on page 157.

Plain Border: Cut borders 3".

You may appliqué a 3/8" finished bias strip around the border of squares and log cabin border.

In some ways I am sad that this is the end of the Round Robin. It has been fun to receive a new block each month for a new challenge. The exciting part is that we will soon see what everyone has done with the blocks. This has been a great experience.

– Paula Kemperman – Belmont, Michigan

OUT ON A LIMB BLOCK

Designed By: Marjorie Nelson - Frankfort, Michigan

Finished size: 6" square

Cut one 6 1/2" background square.

Cut out all of the template pieces. Appliqué the pieces to the background using your favorite technique being sure to add 1/4" seam allowance if you are appliquéing by hand.

After the appliqué work is done, you may want to embellish the bird and leaves with embroidery.

GATHERING FRIENDSHIPS
SIGNATURE QUILT

GATHERING FRIENDSHIPS
SIGNATURE QUILT

Finished size: 33 1/2" x 33 1/2"

Quilt Created By:

Marjorie Nelson - Frankfort, Michigan

The Quilt Recipe:

Center: "Gathering Friendships Signature Blocks" 6" finished block found on page 94.

Triangle Borders: See instructions for setting borders on point found on page 113.

Plain Border: See instructions on "extension borders," found on page 9.

Prairie Point Border: Found on page 178 .

Cut border 3 1/2" x desired length.

Use 1 1/2" squares for prairie points.

Marjorie Nelson made basket blocks for each Round Robin friend to sign.
The blocks traveled with her quilt block. When she got the quilt and the signature blocks back, she made
a wall hanging to celebrate the quilting friendships she had gathered through this experience.

If you would like to have a signature quilt, make all your blocks in advance and let them travel with the center block.

Invite each of the Round Robin participants to sign a block.

GATHERING FRIENDSHIPS
SIGNATURE QUILT

Individual finished block 6" square

Cutting Guide:

For each signature block you will need the following ;

Templates include 1/4" seam allowance.

Plain Yellow:

    Template A: cut two

    Template C: cut two

Basket Fabric:

    Template A: cut one

    Template B: cut two

Handle: cut a bias strip 3/4" x 6 1/2"

Piecing Guide:

Appliqué the basket handle to background A. (Turn under seam allowance.) Piece background A to basket A. Press seam allowance towards the basket. Sew C to B as shown. Press seams towards the dark. Sew these units to the basket sides. Press seam allowance away from the basket. Sew piece A to the bottom of the basket. Press seams towards the triangle.

Have your friends sign the blocks using a permanent Pigma pen. Iron freezer paper to the back of the block for stability when signing. Peel paper away when done.

Sew the blocks together. Use plain blocks for alternating blocks if desired.

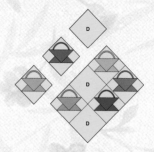

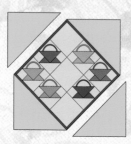

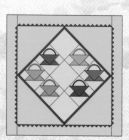

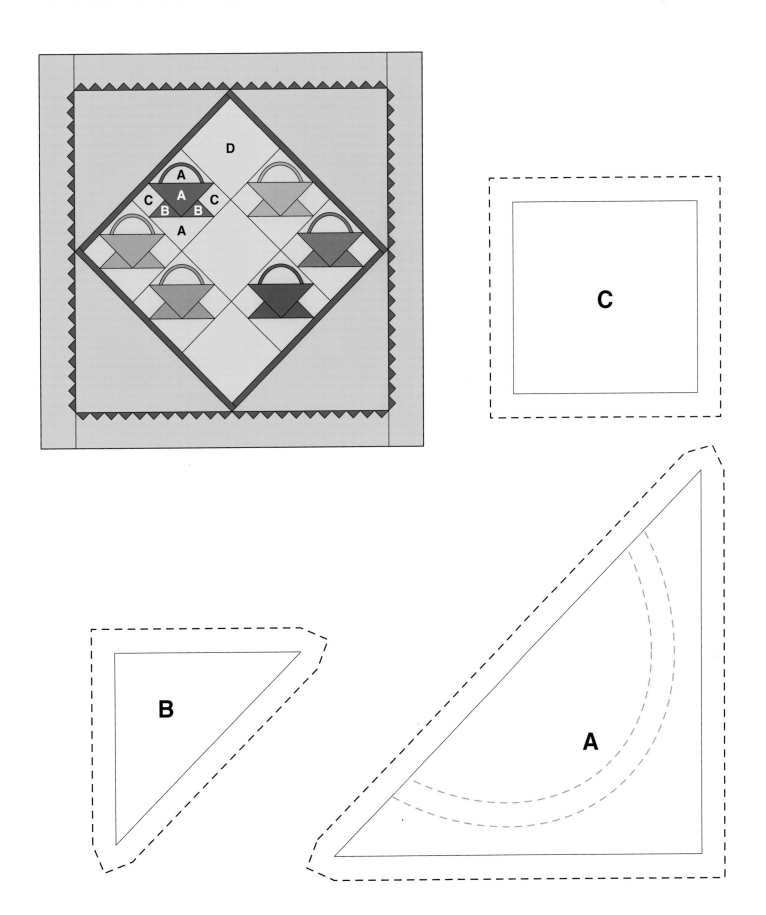

TRIANGLE BORDERS

The quilts fromn left to right are December Night, Ocean of Stars and Rebecca's Flowers.

HOURGLASS & SPLIT HOURGLASS BORDER

Determine the length of the border needed. Divide the length by one of the template sizes listed below. This will tell you the size and number of blocks needed.

HOURGLASS BLOCKS

Finished Size:

Template HG-2 (2"): cut a 3 1/4" square. Cut in half twice on the diagonal.

Template HG-3 (3"): cut a 4 1/4" square. Cut in half twice on the diagonal.

Template HG-3.5 (3 1/2"): cut a 4 3/4" square. Cut in half twice on the diagonal.

Template HG-4 (4"): cut a 5 1/4" square. Cut in half twice on the diagonal.

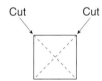

Piece the triangles together as shown. Press the seams towards the darker fabric.

SPLIT HOURGLASS

Finished Block Size:

For a 2" finished block you will need the following:

Template SP-2: cut a 2 7/8" square from the background fabric. Cut it in half once on the diagonal.

Template HG-2: cut two 3 1/4" squares from different fabrics. Cut each square in half twice on the diagonal.

For a 3" finished block you will need the following:

Template SP-3: cut a 3 7/8" square from the background fabric. Cut it in half once on the diagonal.

Template HG-3: cut two 4 1/4" squares from different fabrics. Cut each square in half twice on the diagonal.

Piece the triangles together as shown. Press the seams towards the darker fabric. Press the seams towards the large triangle after it is sewn on.

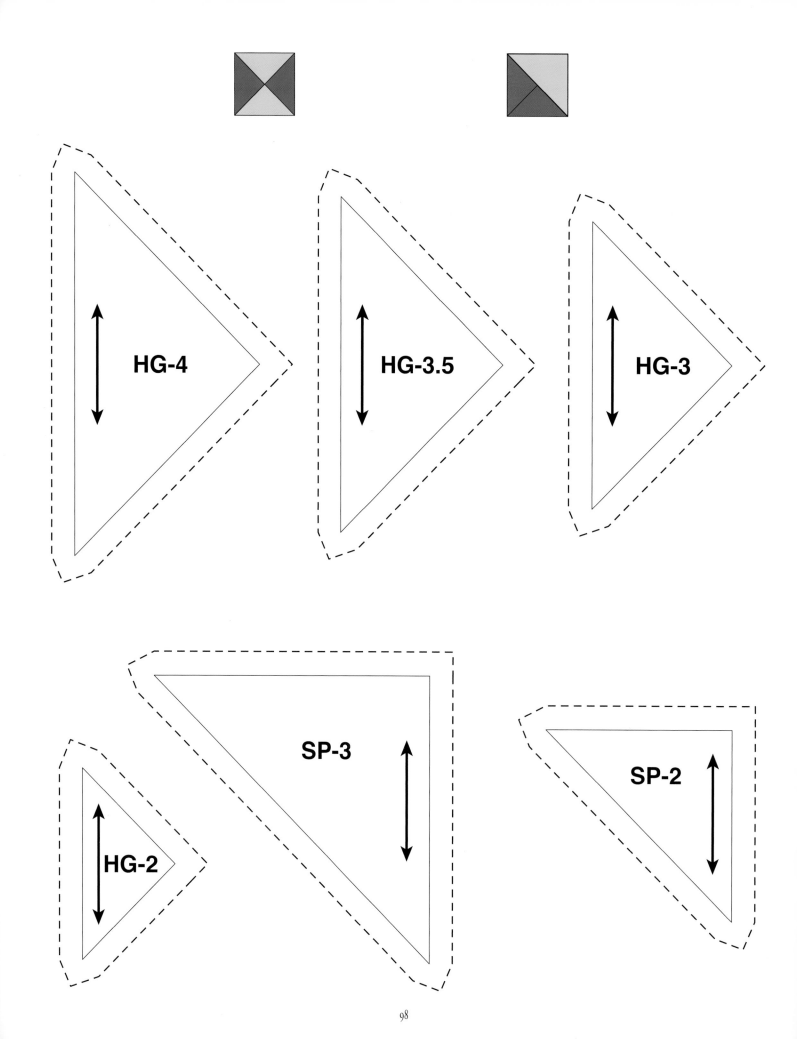

HG-4

HG-3.5

HG-3

HG-2

SP-3

SP-2

FLYING GEESE BORDER

Finished unit size: 4" x 2" by the desired length

All measurements include 1/4" seam allowance

Determine how long you would like your border to be. Divide the number by 2.

This will tell you how many flying geese units you need to make.

For each unit you will need the following:

Background fabric:

Template B: cut a 2 7/8" square Cut in half once on the diagonal.

Main Fabric:

Template A: cut a 5 1/4" square. Cut in half twice on the diagonal.

Sew pieces B to A as shown. Press the seam towards piece B.

Sew the required number of flying geese units together.

Cut 4 squares from the background fabric and sew in the four corners.

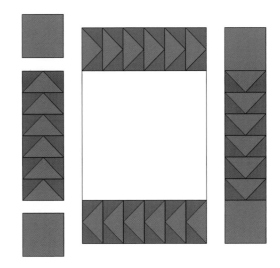

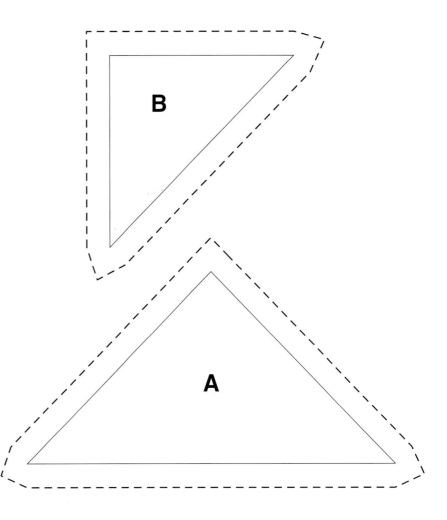

SAWTOOTH STAR BORDER

Sized to fit a 12 1/2" unfinished block.

Measurements include 1/4" seam allowance.

Star Points: Template A: cut four 6 7/8" squares and cut in half once

on the diagonal.

Background B: cut one 13 1/4" square and cut in half twice on the diagonal.

Corner Squares: cut four 6 1/2" squares. Due to page constraints,

no template is given for the corner square designated as Template C.

Piecing Guide:

Sew star points A to the sides of B. Press seam allowances towards the

star points.

Sew two of these units to the top and bottom of the hanging.

Sew the corner squares to each end of the other units. Press towards the

corner squares.

Sew to the sides of the hanging.

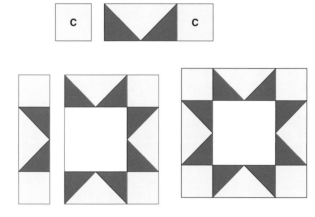

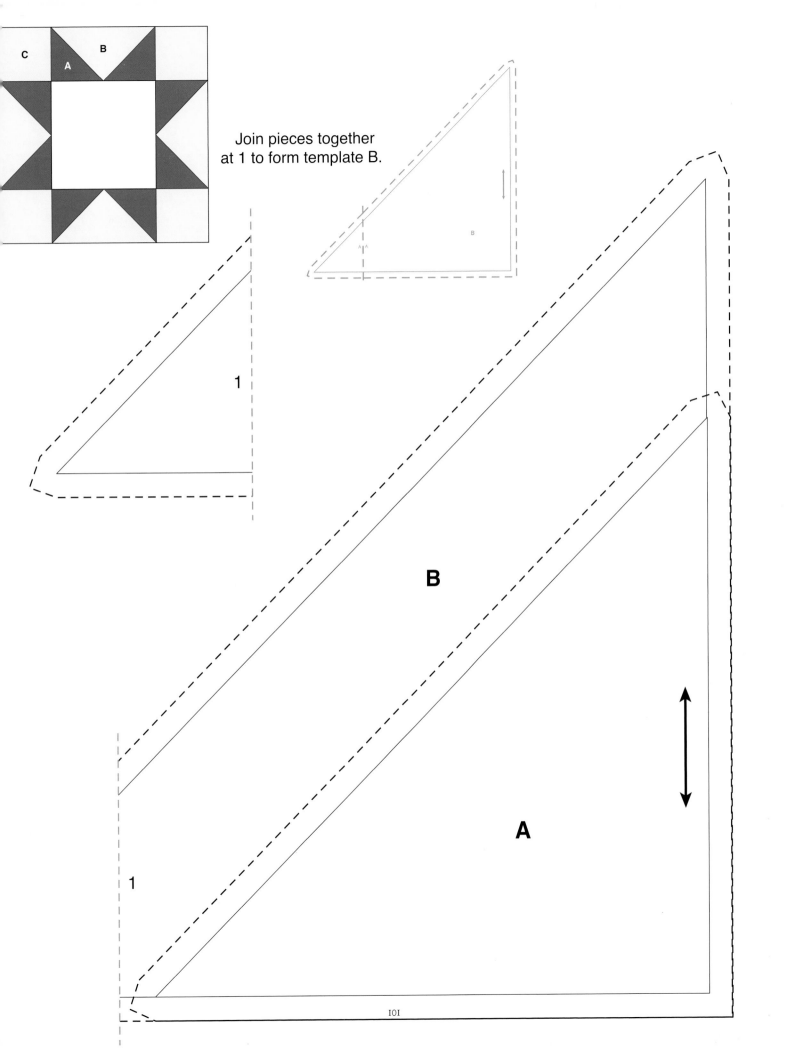

Join pieces together
at 1 to form template B.

1

B

1

A

On Point Sawtooth Border

Sized for a 12 1/2" unfinished block

Measurements include 1/4" seam allowance.

Template A: cut 4

Template B: cut 44 light and 36 dark

Sewing Instructions:

Piece together 36 sawtooth blocks. Press towards the darker fabric.

Sew together 4 sawtooth block units. Press all the seams towards one side. Make four of these units. Sew the sawtooth units to a short side of triangle A. Press the seams towards triangle A. Piece together 5 sawtooth units. Press all seams towards one side. Make four of these units. Sew a light triangle B to one end of this unit.

Sew this unit to the other side of the triangle A unit.

Sew the Sawtooth units to the center block as shown.

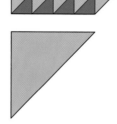

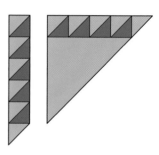

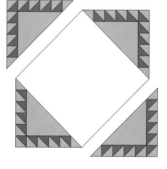

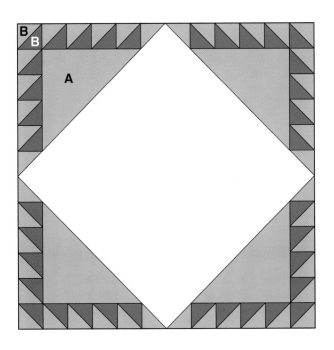

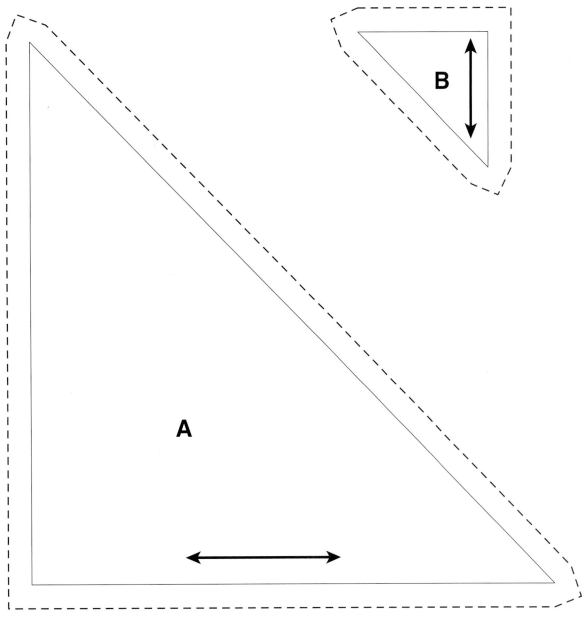

SHARK'S TOOTH BORDER

(Paper Pieced)

Sized for a 12 1/2" unfinished block

Measurements include 1/4" seam allowance

Due to page constraints, you will have to extend the foundation paper. Decide how long your borders need to be. Add extra foundation paper sections until you get the desired length.

SHARK'S TOOTH

Finished 1 1/2" wide x desired length

Background: cut four 2" squares. These will be the corner squares for the borders. A: cut 1 3/4" x 2 1/2" rectangles. Cut enough rectangles for the border lengths.

Triangle fabric: B: cut 1 3/4" x 2 1/2" rectangles. Cut enough rectangles for the border lengths.

OR

Finished 1 3/4" wide x desired length

Background: cut four 2 1/4" squares. These will be the corner squares for the borders. F: cut 2" x 2 3/4" rectangles. Cut enough rectangles for the border lengths.

Triangle fabric: E: cut 2" x 2 3/4" rectangles. Cut enough rectangles for the border lengths.

OR

Finished 2 1/2" wide x desired length

Background: cut four 3" squares. These will be the corner squares for the borders. D: cut 2 1/4" x 3 1/2" rectangles. Cut enough rectangles for the border lengths.

Triangle fabric: C: cut 2 1/4" x 3 1/2" rectangles. Cut enough rectangles for the border lengths.

Paper Piecing Instructions:

Think of paper piecing as sewing by number. You will need to sew on the printed side so the sewing line is facing you. Sew on the solid lines. It's easier to tear the paper off at the end if you use small stitches.

1. With your fingers, make a crease in the paper along the sewing line between piece number 1 and piece number 2. Turn the paper over so the blank side is facing you. Feel for the crease you made. Place the first fabric right side up. Place the next piece of fabric with the right side atop the first fabric. (The back of fabric #2 should be facing you.) While holding the fabric in place, turn the paper over. The printed side should be facing you and the fabrics should be underneath the paper. Sew on the solid line. Trim the seam allowance to 1/4". Press the fabric so both right sides face you. Make a crease on the next sewing line. Place the next fabric with the wrong side facing you. Turn it over and sew on the solid line. Keep repeating the process until you have the border done. Make sure you trim the seam allowance and press as you go.

2. After you are finished, trim the border to a 1/4" seam allowance along the outside edge. Carefully tear the paper off the back.

Next sew the top and bottom border to the hanging.

Sew the corner squares to the side borders.

Sew the side borders to the hanging.

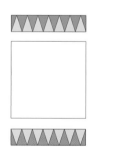

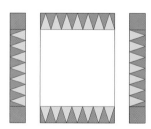

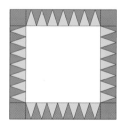

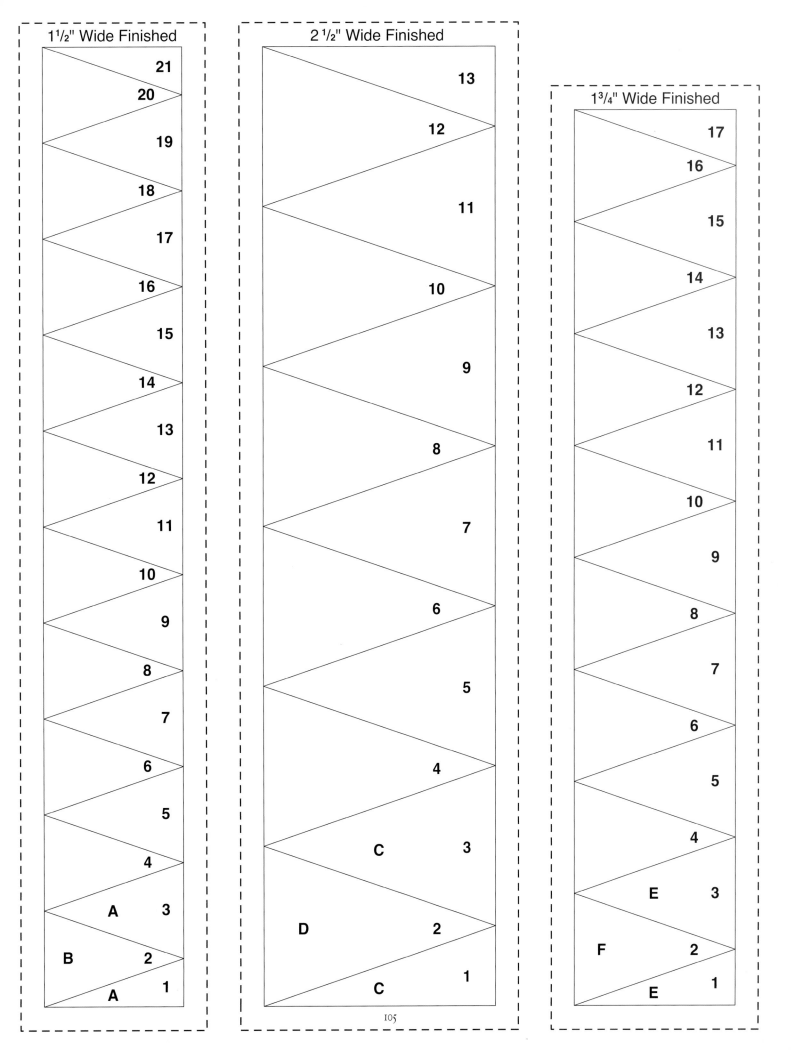

NEW YORK BEAUTY

Finishes 3" x desired length

Measurements include 1/4" seam allowance.

Determine how long you would like your border to be. Divide this number by 6.____ This will tell you how many triangles you will need for your border. Multiply by four to find out how many triangles total you will need.

Side Triangles: Template A: cut one 7 1/4" square. Cut in half twice on the diagonal. Cut the required number of triangles for your borders. You will need background and main triangle fabric.

New York Beauty (Cutting for four corner pieced triangles)
    Background fabric: Template B: Cut 4 pieces.

    Pieced arc: cut 32 rectangles 1 3/4 " x 2 1/4" (background fabric)
                cut 28 rectangles 1 1/2" x 2 1/4" (triangle fabric)

    Fabric of choice: Template D: cut 4 pieces.

Paper pieced arc:

1. With your fingers, make a crease in the paper along the sewing line between piece number 1 and piece number 2.
2. Turn the paper over so the blank side is facing you. Feel for the crease you made. Place the first fabric right side up. Place the next piece of fabric with the right side facing the first fabric. (The back of fabric number 2 should be facing you.) While holding the fabric in place, turn the paper over. The printed side should be facing you and the fabrics should be underneath the paper. Sew on the solid line. Trim the seam allowance to 1/4." Press the fabric so both right sides face you. Make a crease where the next sewing line is. Place the next fabric so the wrong side is facing you. Turn it over and sew on the solid line. Keep

repeating the process until you have the arc done. Make sure you trim the seam allowances and press as you go.

2. After you are finished, trim the border so you have a 1/4" seam allowance along the outside edge. Carefully tear the paper off the back.

Sewing the pieces together:

Place the pieced arc section on top of piece D. Carefully pin and sew. Press towards D. Place piece B on top of the pieced arc section. Carefully pin and sew. Press towards B.

Sew the A triangles together as shown. Sew the triangle borders to the hanging. Sew the top and bottom first. Press. Sew the side borders next. Press. Sew the New York Beauty triangles to the corners. Press.

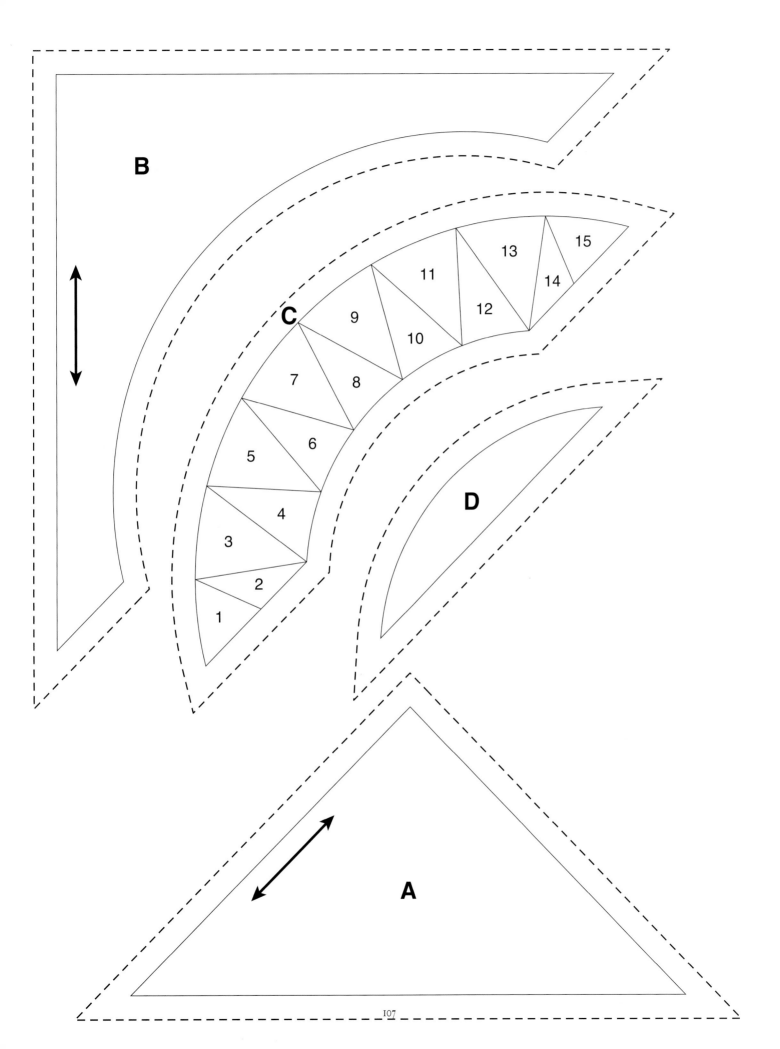

B

C

9
7
8
5
6
3
4
1
2

11
13
15
10
12
14

D

A

SQUARE PATHWAY BORDER

Finishes 1 1/2" wide x desired length

Determine the length of borders needed _____.

Divide this number by 1.5 _____. This will give you the number of blocks you need for the borders_____.

You may need to add an expansion border to make your borders fit.

1/4" seam allowances are included in measurements.

Rotary Cutting Directions:

Center Squares A: cut 1 1/2" squares.

Side Triangles B: cut 2 3/4" squares. Cut in half twice on both diagonals.

(This will yield 4 triangles per square)

Corner Triangles C: cut 1 5/8" squares. Cut in half once on the diagonal.

(This will yield 2 triangles per square)

Piece together the units as shown. Press the seams towards the square.

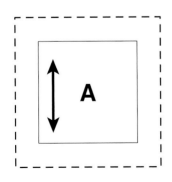

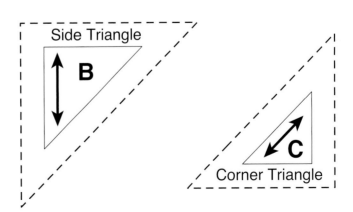

SAWTOOTH BORDER

Finishes 1 1/2" wide x desired length

Measurements include 1/4" seam allowance.

Determine the length of borders needed. Divide the length by one of the template sizes listed below. This will tell you the size and number of the blocks needed.

Finished Size

Template A (1"): cut square 1 7/8." Cut in half once on the diagonal.

Template B (1 1/2"): cut square 2 3/8." Cut in half once on the diagonal.

Template C (2"): cut square 2 7/8." Cut in half once on the diagonal.

Template D (2 1/2"): cut square 3 3/8." Cut in half once on the diagonal.

Template E (3"): cut square 3 7/8." Cut in half once on the diagonal.

Template F (4"): cut square 4 7/8." Cut in half once on the diagonal.

Piece the triangles together according to the diagram. Press the seams towards the darker fabric. Sew the triangle blocks together. Press all block seams to the same side.

Try arranging the blocks in different ways.

If the blocks are turned as shown, one can also make pinwheels.

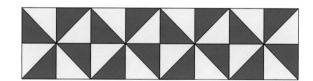

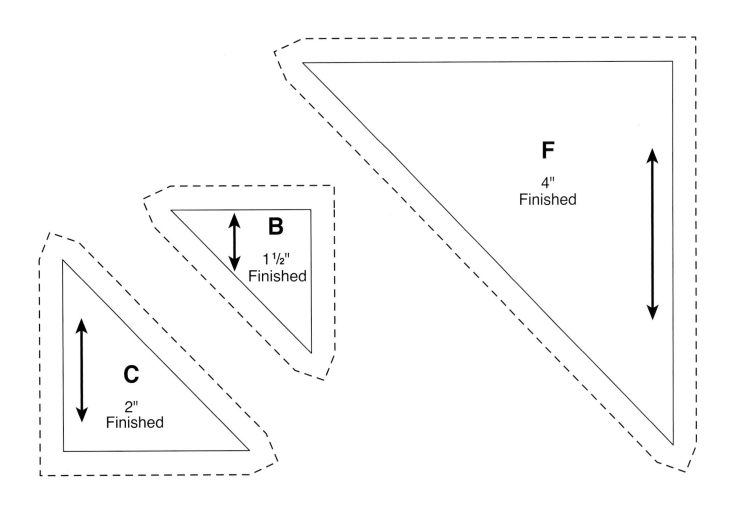

F
4"
Finished

B
1½"
Finished

C
2"
Finished

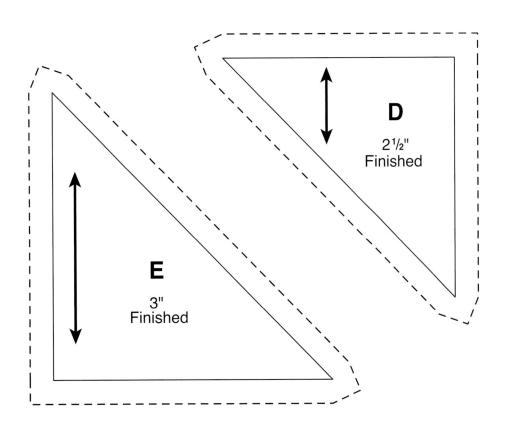

D
2½"
Finished

E
3"
Finished

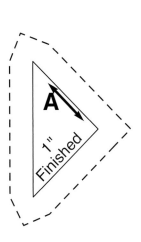

A
1"
Finished

BUTTERFLIES IN FLIGHT BORDER

Finished border size: 2" x the desired length.

Measurements include 1/4" seam allowance.

Determine how long your borders need to be._____

Divide that number by 2._____

This will tell you how many units you need for one strip of the border. You will

need to sew two of these strips together to make the border for one side.

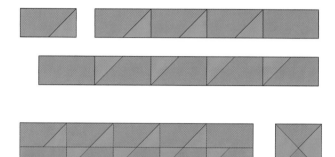

From the background fabric: cut the required number of rectangles 1 1/2" x 2 1/2".

Subtract the number 8 from the required number of rectangles. This is the

number of squares you need for the borders.

From the triangle fabric, cut the required number of squares 1 1/2" x 1 1/2".

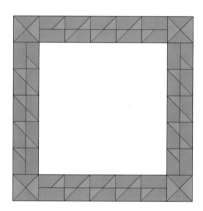

Place 1 square on the corners of the rectangles with the right sides together.

Sew from corner to corner on the diagonal. Trim the excess fabric away and leave

a 1/4" seam allowance. Press the seam towards the background fabric.

Sew the butterfly units together as shown.

Make four 2" finished hourglass blocks for the border corners. Directions found

on page 97.

TRIANGLE SPIRES ON POINT

Fits a 6" or 12" finished block

All measurements include 1/4" seam allowance.

Cutting instructions for 6" finished block.

      Background: Template B-6: cut 8

      Triangle Spires: Template A-6: cut 4

Cutting Instructions for a 12" finished block.

      Background: Template B-12: cut 8

      Triangle Spires: Template A-12: cut 4

Piecing instructions for both sizes:

Sew piece B to piece A. Press seam allowance towards B. Then sew piece B

to the other side of A. Press seam allowance towards B. Make four of these units.

Sew the triangle units to the center block as shown.

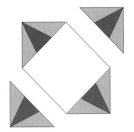

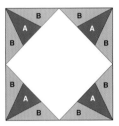

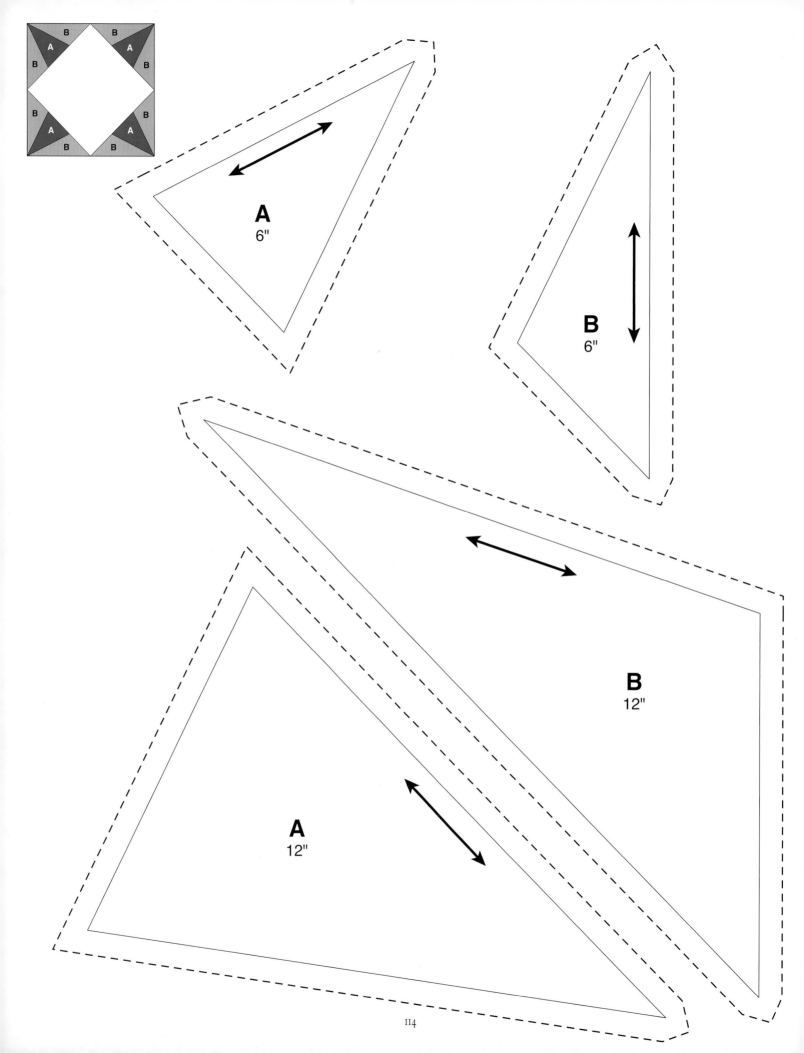

A
6"

B
6"

B
12"

A
12"

PLAIN BORDERS

Wind, Sand and Sky:
A Day at the Lake

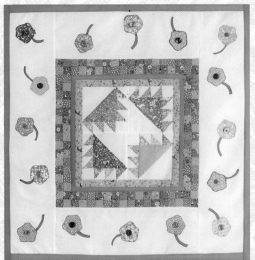

Ring Around the Posies

Out on a Limb

SHOOTING STARS BORDER

Designed by: Gerd Villadsen - Molde, Norway

Finished 3 1/4" x desired length

Decide how long you want the border to be. Cut the borders 3 3/4" x this measurement.

Sew the top and bottom borders to the hanging and press. Next sew the side borders on and press.

Stars:

Template A: cut ten. Use your favorite method of appliqué. Add 1/4" seam allowance if appliquéing by hand.

Template B: cut two. Use your favorite method of appliqué and add 1/4" seam allowance if appliquéing by hand.

Appliqué the stars to the border as desired.

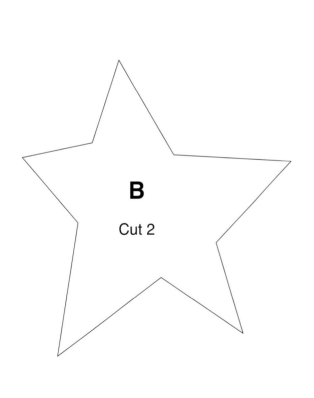

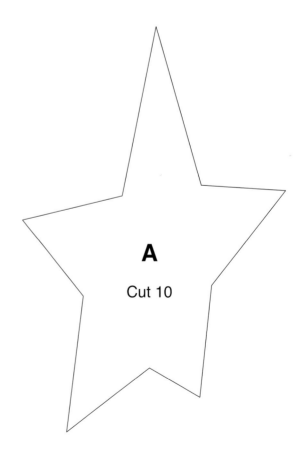

FRAMED BORDER

Designed by: Ardie Sveadas - Sparta, Michigan

Measurements include 1/4" seam allowance.

Cut the top and side borders 1" x desired length. Cut the bottom border 1 3/4" x desired length.

Sew the top and bottom borders to the hanging. Press the seams towards the outside of border.

Sew the side borders on. Press the seams towards the outside borders. Add 1/4" seam allowance to the appliqué pieces. Appliqué the boards on an angle at the bottom.

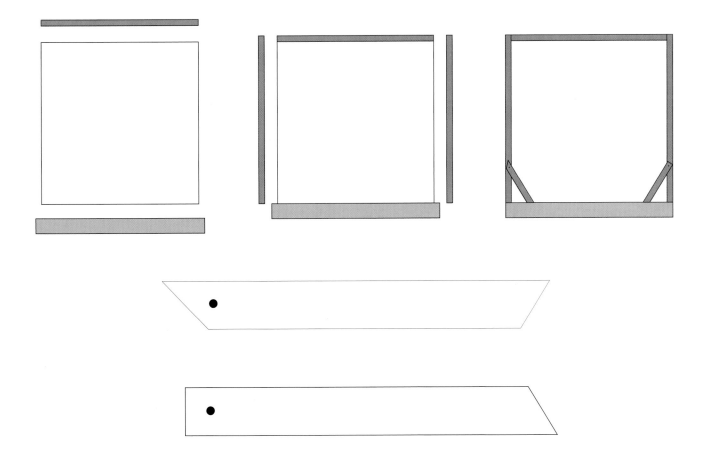

FENCE BORDER

Designed by: Lois Lewis - Boyne City, Michigan
Finished 2" x desired length

All measurements include 1/4" seam allowance.

Figure out how long the border needs to be.

Fence Units:

Fence fabric:

> Template A: cut 16 pieces 3/4" x 2 1/2"
>
> Template C: cut 24 pieces 3/4" x 2"

Background Fabric:

> Template B: cut 24 pieces 3/4" x 2"
>
> Template D: cut 12 pieces 1 1/2" x 2"

Corner Squares: cut 4 2 1/2" squares

Piece the units together as shown. Press the seams towards one side.

Sew 3 fence sections together. The block should measure 5 3/4."

To determine the remaining length needed:

Take the desired border measurement._____ Subtract 5.5" from that measurement._____

Add 1/4" seam allowance to one end._____ This is the size needed to cut the remaining border sections. Cut 4 pieces 2 1/2" x this measurement from the background fabric. Sew to the fence sections.

Narrow border:

Cut six 1" wide strips x the length of the fence border. Sew to the top and bottom of the two borders. Sew borders to the top and bottom of the hanging. Cut 4 pieces 1" x 2 1/2." Sew to the ends of the other two borders. Sew the remaining two 1" wide borders to one side of the other two borders. Add the corner squares to the ends of these borders. Press the seams towards the squares. Measure the length of the fence border with the squares on the end. Cut two borders 1" wide by this measurement. Sew to the remaining sides. Refer to the diagram for the sewing arrangement.

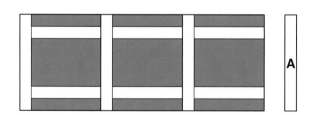

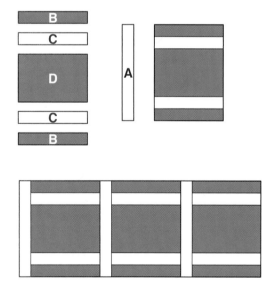

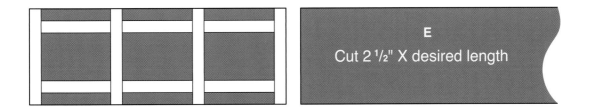

ALTERNATE METHOD

To strip piece the fence sections, cut two background strips 3/4" x 26" and two light strips (fence fabric) 3/4" x 26". Cut one strip of background fabric 1 1/2" x 26." Sew the strips together as shown in the diagram and cut into 2" increments. You will have 2" of excess fabric for straightening purposes. Follow the rest of the directions from this point.

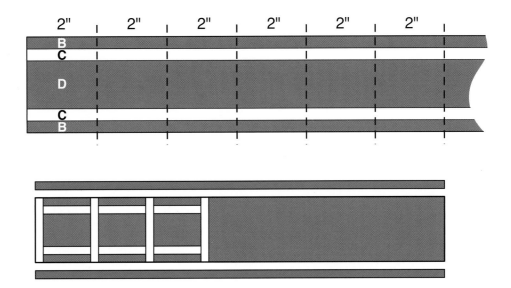

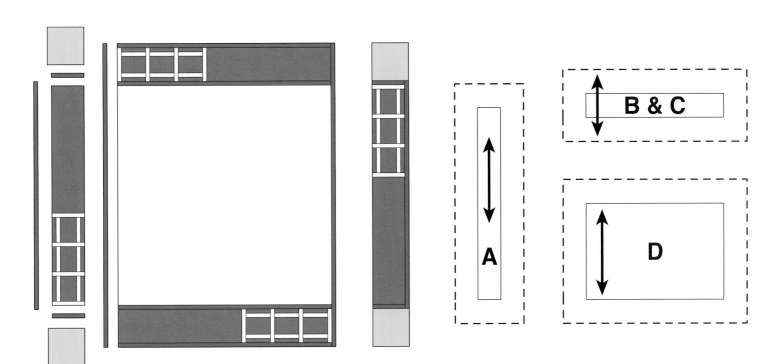

Appliqué Borders

The quilts from left to right are Bell Flower Locally Grown, Basket in the Middle and Winter Solstice.

Norwegian Rosemale

Designed by: Marjorie Nelson - Frankfort Michigan

Finished Size: 5 3/4" x desired length

Use your favorite appliqué technique and add 1/4" seam allowance if appliquéing by hand.

Cut the background 6 1/4" wide by the desired length.

Rosemale design: fold the Rosemale fabric in half. Place the template on the fold and cut out four of the design.

Pin the appliqué in the center of the borders and sew in place.

Place on Fold

DRAGONFLIES IN FLIGHT

Designed by: Paula Kemperman - Belmont, Michigan

Finished size: 3 3/4" x desired length

Use your favorite appliqué technique and add 1/4" seam allowance if appliquéing by hand.

Cut the following:

Border Background: 4 1/2" wide by desired length.

Green Fabric:

>Template A: cut 4

>Template B: cut 4

>Template C: cut 1

>Template D: cut 1

>Template E: cut 1

Berry fabric:

>Template F: cut 24

Dragonflies:

>Template G: cut 8 bodies

>Template H: cut 8 and 8 reversed

>Template I: cut 8 and 8 reversed

Arrange appliqué pieces on borders as desired.

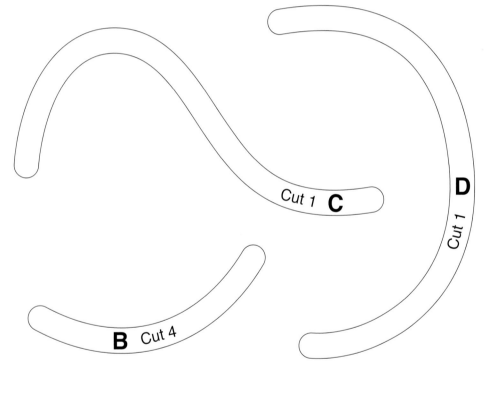

Cut 1 **C**

D Cut 1

E Cut 1

B Cut 4

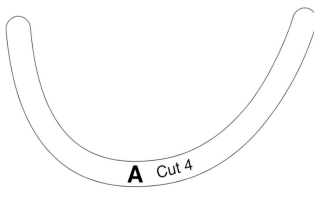

A Cut 4

F
Cut 24

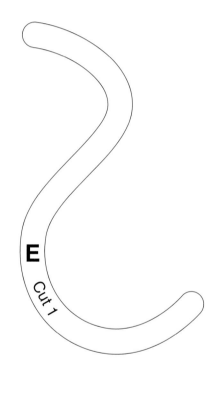

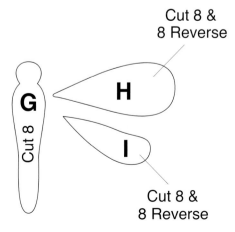

Cut 8 &
8 Reverse

G **H**

Cut 8

I

Cut 8 &
8 Reverse

STAR BLOOMS BORDER

Designed by: Linda Hamel - Frankfort, Michigan

Finished: 6 3/4" x desired length

Use your favorite appliqué technique and add 1/4" seam allowance to appliqué pieces if you are appliquéing by hand.

Flowers: cut 1 each of templates A and B.

Flower Buds: cut one template H

cut 2 of template G

cut 1 of template I

Green fabric:

Leaves: cut 2 and 2 reverse of template J

Calyx: Template C: cut 1

Template E: cut 2

Template F: cut 1

Vine: cut 4 bias strips: 7/8" x 15 1/2"

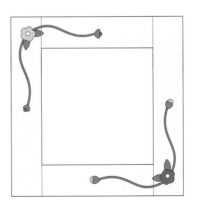

Flower Centers: cut 2 each template D.

Background Fabric: cut 7 1/4" wide by desired length.

Appliqué the pieces to the background fabric.

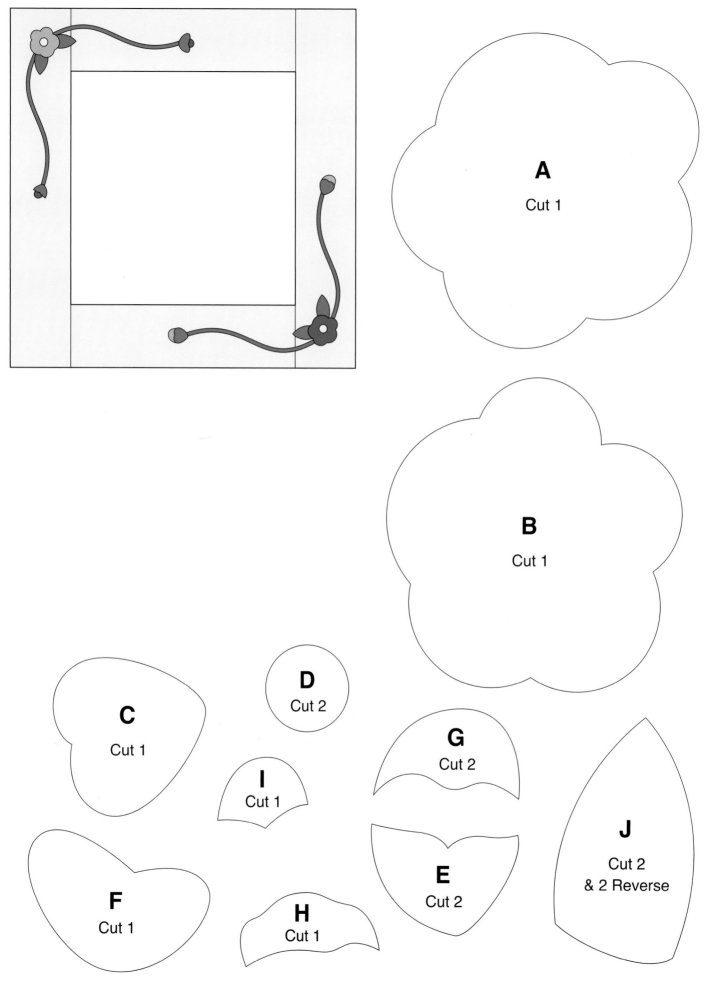

HOLLY BERRY BORDER

Designed by: Jackie Huizen - Hudsonville, Michigan

Finished Size: 2 3/4" x the desired length

Use your favorite appliqué technique and add 1/4" seam allowance if appliquéing by hand.

Background fabric: cut 3 1/4" wide by the desired length.

Vine: cut and piece together enough 1" bias strips to yield a piece that is 86" long or desired length. Use the layout as a placement guide.

Berries: cut and appliqué 24 berries in place.

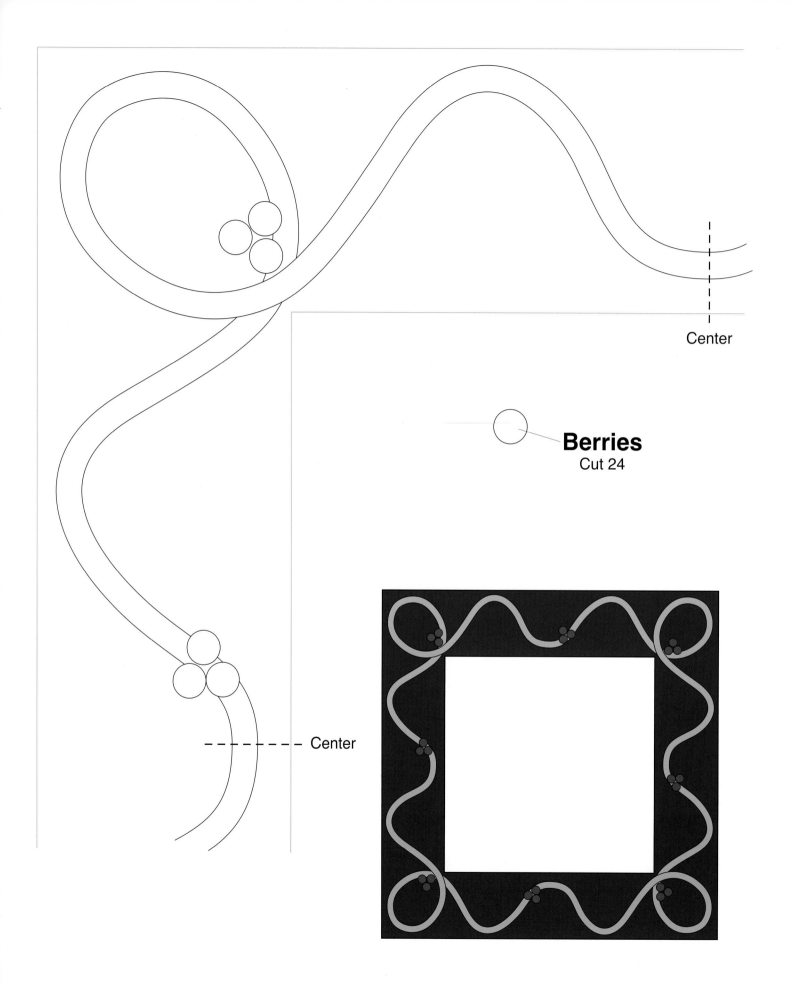

Center

Berries
Cut 24

Center

SIGNS OF SPRING

Designed by: Susan Rand - Rockford, Michigan

Finished Size: 6" x desired length

The flowers are pieced and then appliquéd to the background. If you are appliquéing by hand, add 1/4" seam allowance.

Flower 1: cut out templates A, B and C. Piece together as shown. Make four flowers.

Flower 2: cut out templates D, E, and F. Piece together as shown. Make four flowers.

Flower 3: cut out templates G and H. Appliqué the bud as shown. Make four flowers.

Flower 4: cut out templates J and K. Sew K to all four sides of J. Press the seams towards the center. Make four flowers.

Circles: cut 16.

Leaves: cut 28 (add seam allowance).

Vines: make bias strips that will finish 1/4" x 31." See the directions on making bias strips on page 12.

Appliqué all pieces to the background.

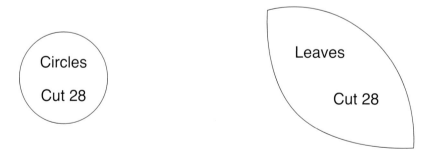

Circles

Cut 28

Leaves

Cut 28

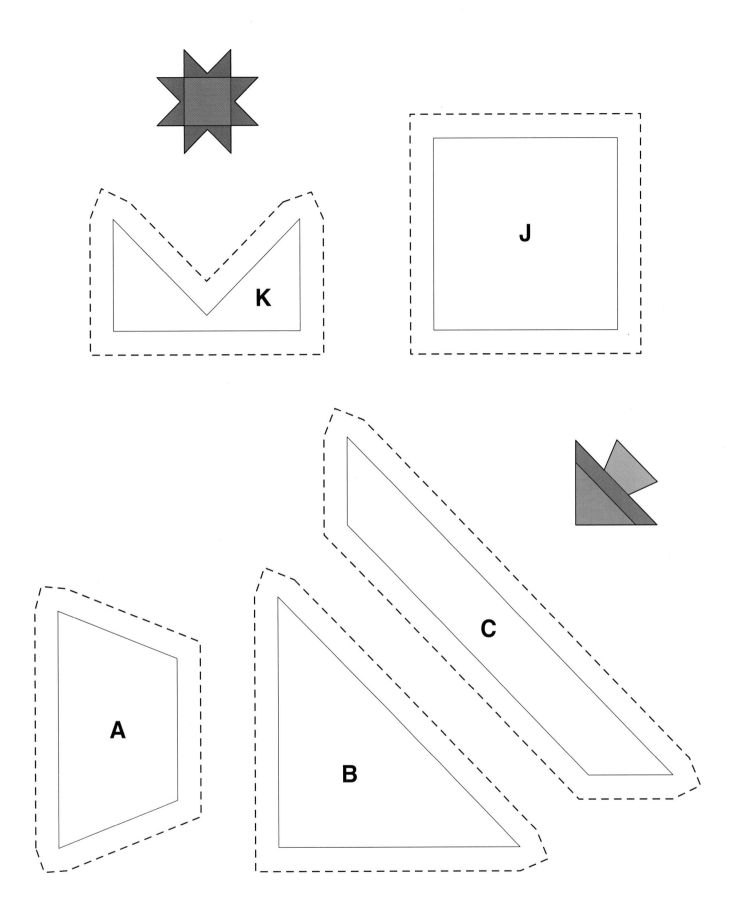

K

J

C

A

B

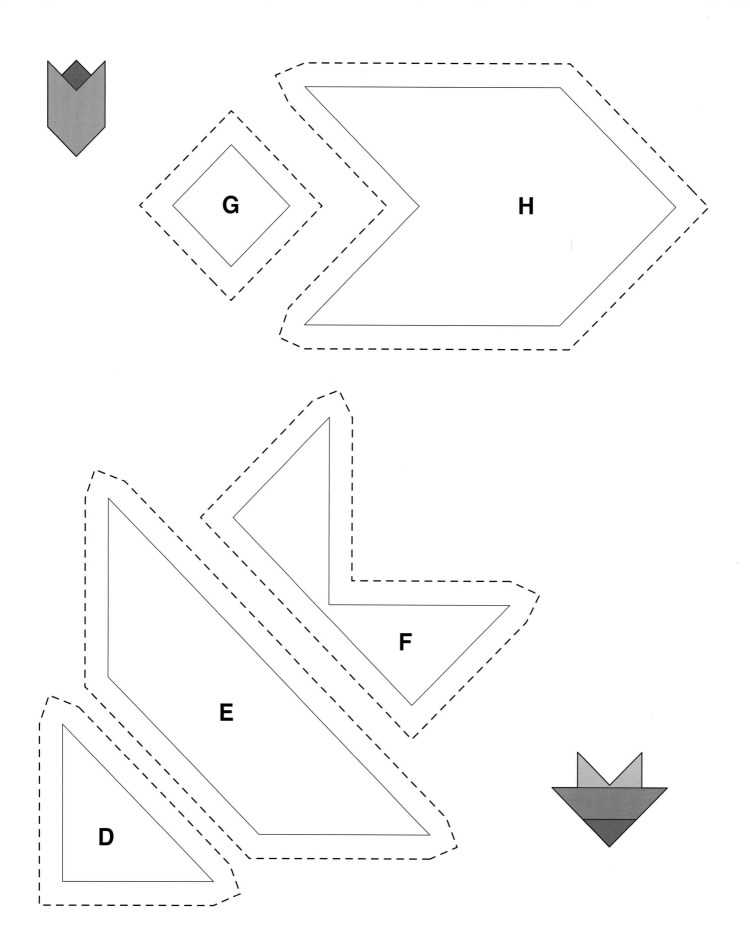

STARRY PATH VARIATION

Designed by: Jo Black Danford - Beulah, Michigan

Finished size: 5 3/4" x desired length

Use your favorite appliqué method and add 1/4" seam allowance if appliquéing by hand.

Cut the background: 6 1/4" x desired length.

Stars: cut four of Starry Path Variation template B

cut thirteen of Starry Path Variation template C

cut two of Starry path variation template A.

Vine Path: a decorative thread was used for the path between the stars. Zigzag over the decorative thread with invisible or matching thread.

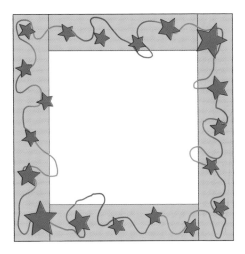

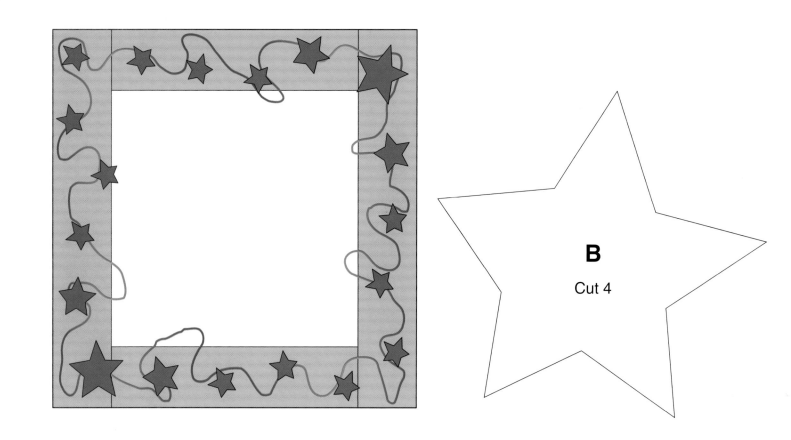

B

Cut 4

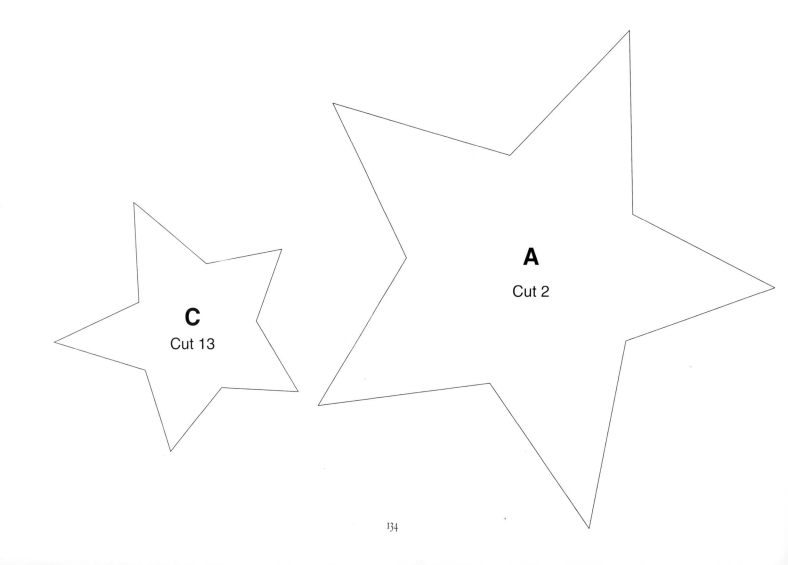

A

Cut 2

C

Cut 13

FLORAL GARLAND

Designed by: Emilie Kimpel - Arcadia, Michigan

Finished Size: 2 3/4" x desired length

Border background: Cut 3 1/4" x the desired length.

Vines: cut 1/4" finished bias strips.

Leaves: some of the leaves on this border are three-dimensional. To make dimensional leaves follow the directions below. Otherwise, appliqué the leaves to the background using your favorite appliqué technique.

Dimensional Leaves:

Template A: cut two 9" squares. Iron a piece of fusible web between the two layers of fabric. Cut twenty-one leaves out of this piece.

Template B: follow the same directions for Template A. Cut twenty-one leaves.

Machine sew with a straight stitch around the edges of the dimensional leaves before you sew them to the hanging. This will help prevent the layers from coming apart with time. Sew the leaves up the center to attach them to the hanging. It should look like a leaf vein.

Gathered Roses:

Large Rose: cut five strips 1 1/8" x 18"

Medium Rose: cut three strips 1 1/8" x 15"

Half Rose: cut three strips 1 1/8" x 6"

Press 1/4" to the wrong sides of the strips. Start at the top left side and mark 1" increments along the length of the strip. On the bottom right side make a

mark 1/2" in from one end. Then mark the rest of the side in 1" increments.

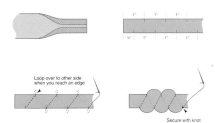

Hand stitch in a zigzag pattern from one mark to the next mark. When you get to an edge, take the stitch over the top of the edge to the other side. Your stitches should be loose so that the fabric can be gathered. At each three intervals, gently gather the fabric and secure with two or three stitches. Continue in the same manner until you reach the end of the strip. Secure it with a knot.

Turn the strip to form a petal. Hide the edge of the strip under the first petal and secure at the bottom with a couple of stitches. Form five petals and secure at the bottom with a stitch each time you form a petal. Hold the rest of the strip under the petals that are formed. Make more petals and secure them with a stitch as you go. After the flower is formed, tuck the end under the flower. Appliqué the flowers to the background. Sew French knots or add seed beads to the center of the flower.

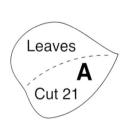

Leaves

A

Cut 21

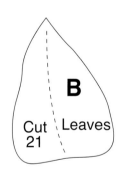

B

Cut
21　Leaves

Sew around edges

Sew along center line
to attach to hanging

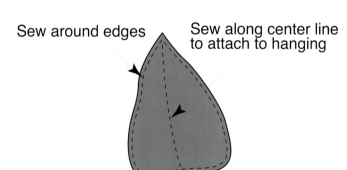

CHERRY BLOSSOM BORDER

Designed by: Anne Grete Nakken - Molde, Norway

Finished size: 3 1/2" x desired length

Use your favorite method of appliqué and add 1/4" seam allowance if appliquéing by hand.

Leaves: cut the number of leaves indicated on the leaf templates.

Gathered Flowers:

Template A: cut thirty-five. Use a small running stitch and turn under 1/8" to the wrong side. Gently gather the stitches towards the center to form a yo-yo. Make a knot.

Divide the circle into five sections and mark.

With the needle going down through the center and up over the side of the flower and back down through the center, gently gather. Repeat for the next

four marks and fasten off on the back. Appliqué the flowers to the top of the quilt.

Make three French knots in the center of the flower.

For placement purposes, see the photo on page 46.

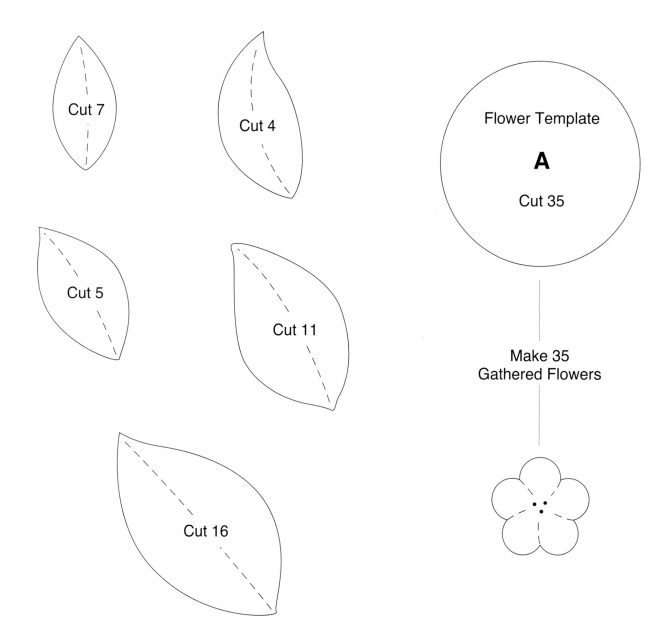

Cut 7

Cut 4

Cut 5

Cut 11

Cut 16

Flower Template

A

Cut 35

Make 35
Gathered Flowers

Seasons of Trees

Designed by: Cindy Larson - Frankfort, Michigan

Finished size: 4" x desired length

Use fusible web and either hand buttonhole or machine appliqué pieces to the border.

Cut the border background: 4 1/2" x desired length.

Trees: join Template A to Template B. Cut out four trees.

Spring tree:

> Green: Template I: cut 8
>
> Template H: cut 4
>
> Template E: cut 2
>
> Bud: Template G: cut 4

Summer tree:

> Flowers: Template J: cut 4
>
> Flower Center: Template K: cut 4
>
> Green: Template F: cut 12
>
> Template D: cut 2

Autumn:

> Leaf: Template C: cut 6

Corner motifs: cut 1 each of sun, moon, leaf and snowflake.

Cut a 4 1/2" background square for corners.

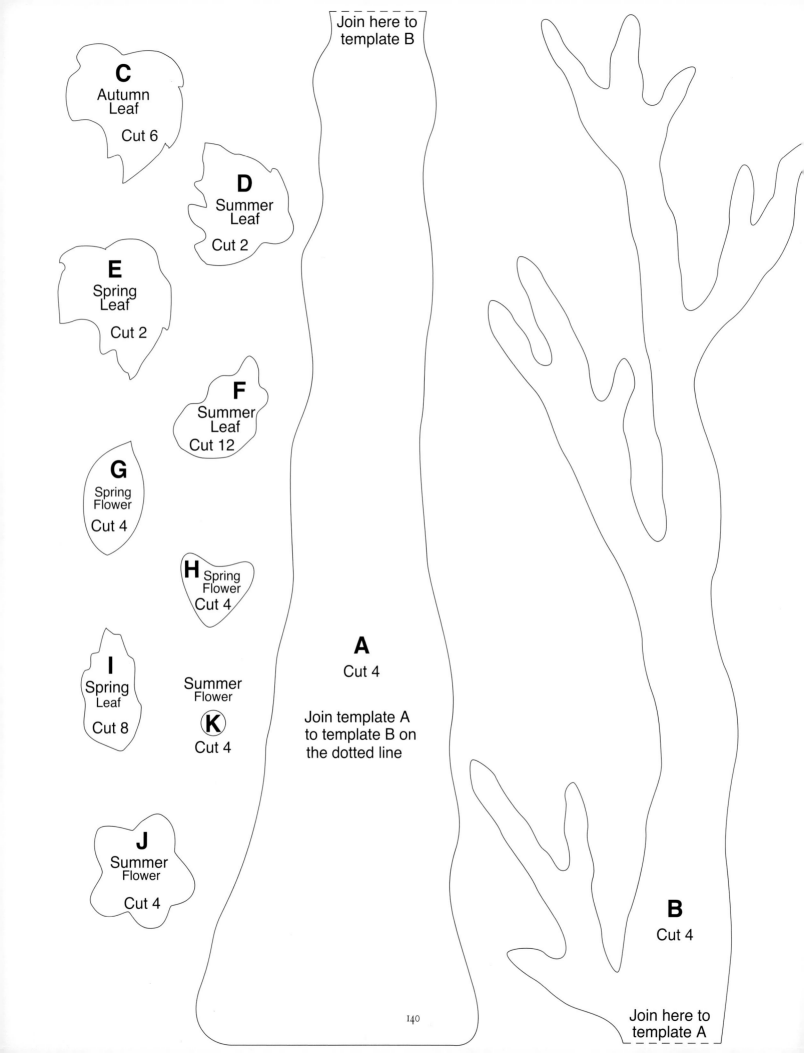

C
Autumn
Leaf

Cut 6

D
Summer
Leaf

Cut 2

E
Spring
Leaf

Cut 2

F
Summer
Leaf
Cut 12

G
Spring
Flower
Cut 4

H Spring
Flower
Cut 4

I
Spring
Leaf

Cut 8

Summer
Flower
K
Cut 4

J
Summer
Flower

Cut 4

Join here to
template B

A

Cut 4

Join template A
to template B on
the dotted line

140

B

Cut 4

Join here to
template A

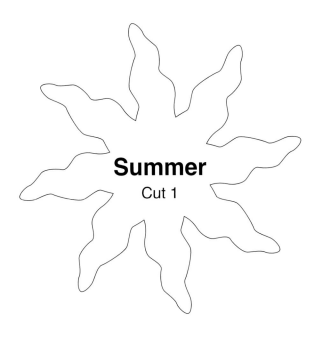

Summer
Cut 1

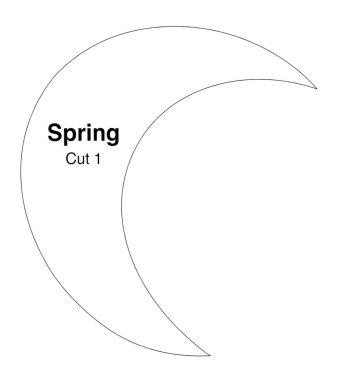

Spring
Cut 1

Autumn
Cut 1

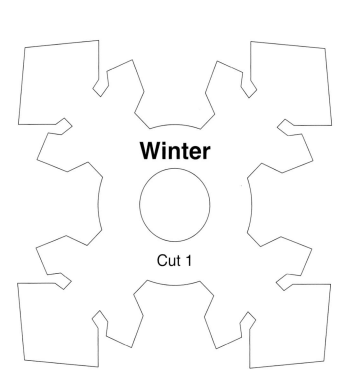

Winter

Cut 1

BUTTON FLOWER

Designed by: Nancy Conrad - Frankfort, Michigan

Finished size: 6" x the desired length.

Use your favorite appliqué technique and add 1/4" seam allowance if appliquéing by hand.

Border background: cut 6 1/2" wide by desired length.

Flowers: cut 16 flowers in a variety of colors.

Stems: cut 16.

Place the pieces on the border as desired and appliqué.

Sew a button in the center of each flower.

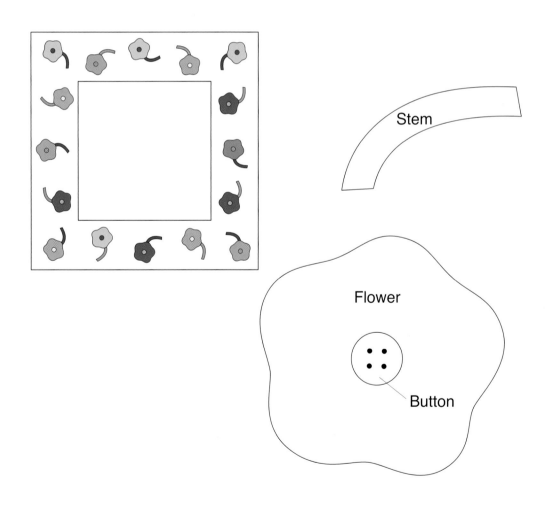

STARRY PATH BORDER

Designed by: Marjorie Nelson - Frankfort, Michigan

Finished size: 6" x the desired length

Use your favorite appliqué method and add 1/4" seam allowance if appliquéing by hand.

Background: cut 6 1/2" x desired length.

Stars: cut 17 of Starry Path Template A. Place on the border as desired.

Vine Path: make enough 1/4" finished bias vine to go around the quilt.

You may weave decorative thread in and out of the appliqué pieces.

Zigzag over the decorative thread with invisible or matching thread..

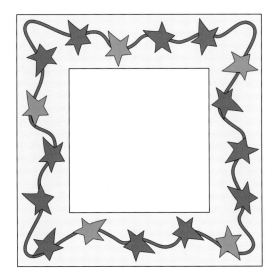

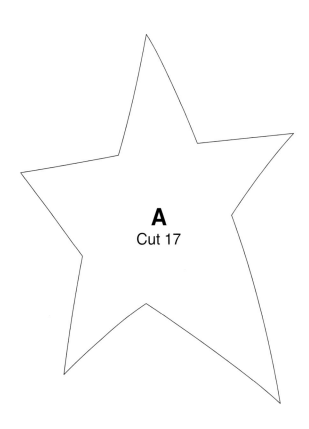

A
Cut 17

CELTIC CABLES

Designed By: Marjorie Nelson - Frankfort, Michigan

Finished Size: 3" x desired length

Cut background fabric 3 1/2" x the desired length.

Make enough 1/4" finished bias tape to sew around the borders. The directions are on page 12.

Use the placement guide for the cables. Repeat the pattern until you have enough to fill the length of your border. Appliqué to the background fabric.

Dimensional Butterfly:

Cut two rectangles 2" x 3". Iron a piece of fusible web to the wrong side of one rectangle. Peel the paper off. Iron the other rectangle to the side that has the fusible web. You should end up with one rectangle with fusible web sandwiched between the two layers. Cut the butterfly wings from this piece. Machine sew around the edges of the wings using a straight stitch. This will prevent the layers from coming apart.

Cut the butterfly body out of a fused piece of fabric.

Place the wings under the body. Sew around the body. The wings will only be attached in place by the body. It should look as if the butterfly is in flight.

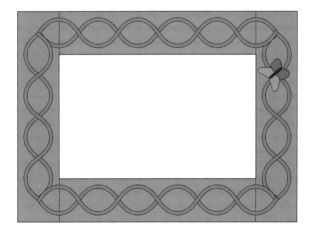

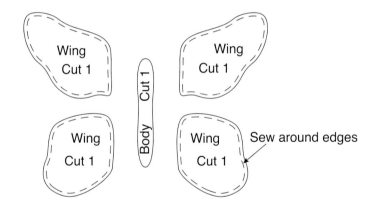

FLOWER PATH BORDER

Designed by: Rebecca Nelson-Zerfas - Beulah, Michigan

Finished size: 5" x desired length

Use your favorite method of appliqué and add 1/4" seam
allowances to pieces if appliquéing by hand.

Cutting Requirements:

      Flowers: cut eight blue and eight pink.

      Leaves: cut sixteen green.

      Vines: cut eight.

Appliqué all pieces to the background.

Leaf
Cut 16

Vine Cut 8

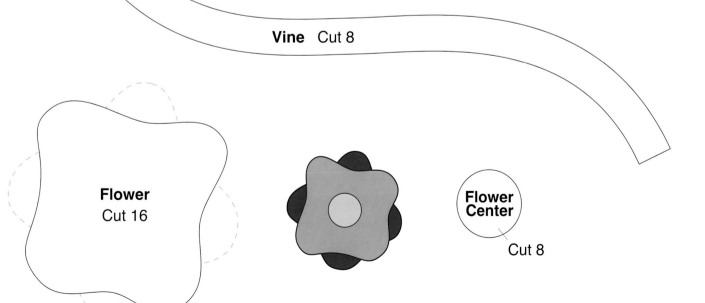

Flower
Cut 16

Flower Center

Cut 8

FLOWERS OF NORWAY

Designed by: Ardie Sveadas - Sparta, Michigan

Finished size: 5 1/2" x the desired length.

Use your favorite appliqué technique and add 1/4" seam allowance if appliquéing by hand.

Border Background: cut 6" wide by the desired length

Long Stem: cut 2 pieces 1" x 5 1/2". Turn under the seam allowance on the sides.

Leaves: cut 20 Template A.

Stems: cut 8 Template F, cut 4 Template G

Flowers: cut 2 Template B, 2 Template C, 2 Template D, 2 Template E Center and appliqué the design to the middle of two borders.

Layout for flowers: Appliqué in this order starting with piece B on the bottom and the rest applied in the following order: C, D, E.

Berries: cut 16 of Template H.

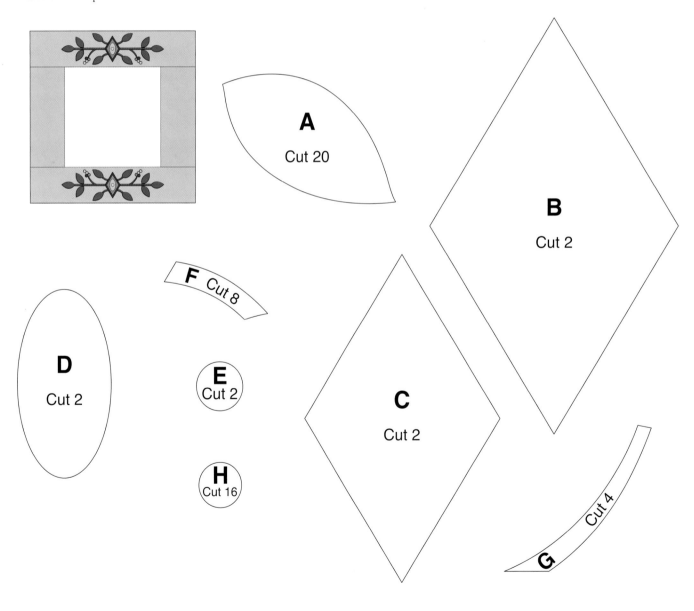

PRIMROSE BORDER

Designed by: Marjorie Nelson - Frankfort, Michigan

Finished Size: 3" x the desired length

Use your favorite appliqué method. Add 1/4" seam allowance if appliquéing by hand.

Border background fabric: Cut at least 3 1/2" wide by desired length.

Cut 8 flower centers from Template A

Cut 8 flowers from Template B

Cut 28 leaves out of Template C

Cut 2 vines from Template D

Cut 2 vines from Template E

Center vines D in the middle of the top and bottom borders.

Center vines E in the middle of the side borders.

Next appliqué the flowers and leaves.

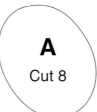

A Cut 8

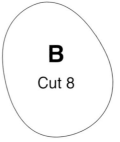

B Cut 8

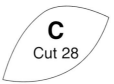

C Cut 28

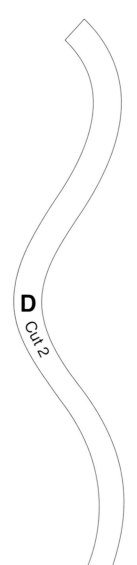

D Cut 2

E Cut 2

PICTURE FRAME BORDER

Designed by: Ardie Sveadas - Sparta, Michigan

Finished size: 2 3/4" x the desired length.

Use your favorite method to appliqué . Add 1/4" seam allowance if hand appliquéing.

Border background: cut 3 1/4" x desired length. Sew the borders to the hanging before the appliqué is put on.

Picture Frame: simply add length in the middle of the template if you need to make this longer. Make sure that you enlarge the square if you make the border longer.

Cut a 14" square piece of fabric and fold it in half once. Fold it in half again. Pin the template on the two folds. Cut out the design. You should have one piece when you open up your design. Appliqué this onto the border.

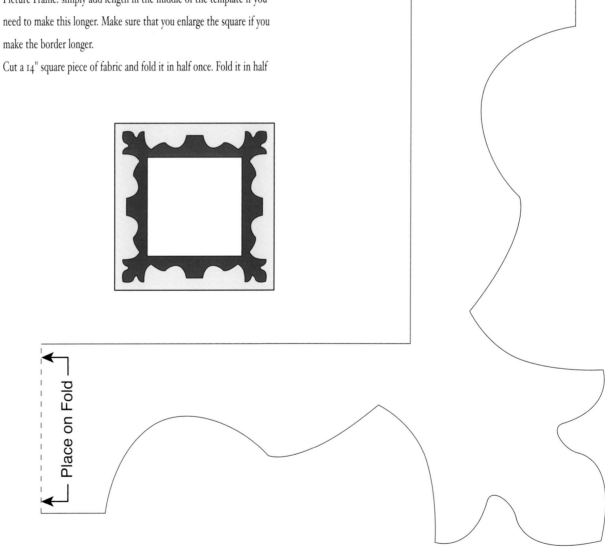

Stars on Point Border

Created by: Vera Sandnes - Molde, Norway

Fits a 20 1/2" unfinished square

Cutting requirements: cut two 15" squares and cut in half once on the diagonal.

Use your favorite appliqué method and appliqué a star in each of the four corners. Remember to add 1/4" seam allowance if you appliqué by hand.

Sew the triangles to opposite sides of the square. Press the seam allowance towards the triangles. Sew the other two triangles to the remaining sides. Press the seams towards the triangles.

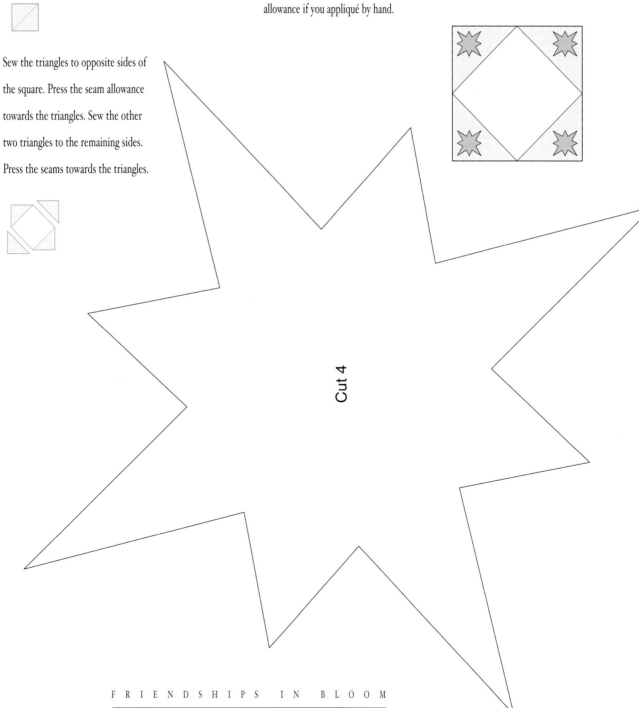

Cut 4

HEARTS ABOUND

Designed by: Solfrid Norvik - Syvde, Norway

Finished size: 3" x the desired length

Use your favorite appliqué method and add 1/4" seam allowance if appliquéing by hand.

Cut the background piece 3" wide by desired length.

Cut out the hearts and appliqué them to the border.

Cut 4

Cut 4

Cut 2

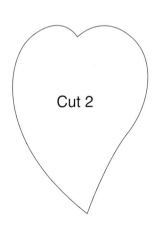

Cut 2

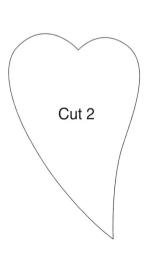

Cut 2

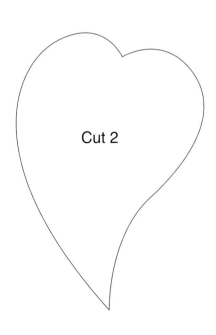

Cut 2

TRIMMING THE TREE

Designed by: Rebecca Nelson-Zerfas - Beulah, Michigan

Finished size: 3 1/4" x desired length

Use your favorite appliqué method and add 1/4" seam allowance if appliquéing by hand.

Cut the background piece 3 3/4" x desired length.

Appliqué all pieces to background.

Embroider the light strand and lights.

You might find a mini strand of lights and other embellishments at your favorite quilt or craft store.

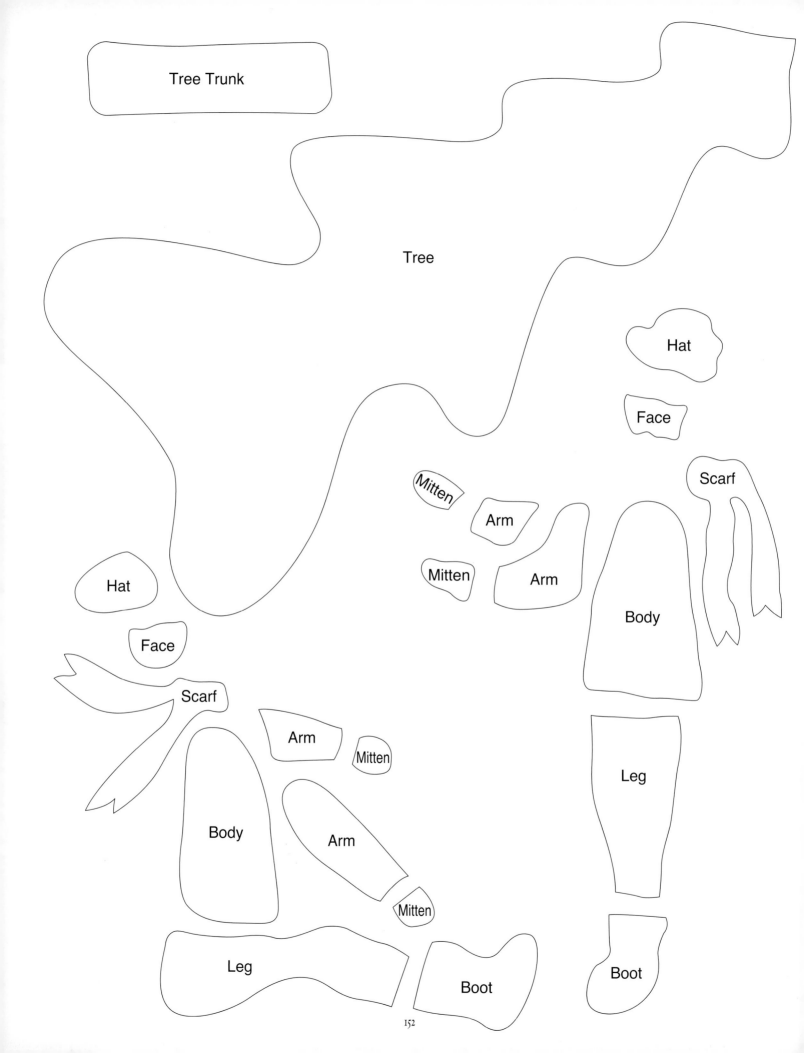

Tree Trunk

Tree

Hat

Face

Scarf

Mitten

Arm

Mitten

Arm

Body

Hat

Face

Scarf

Arm

Mitten

Body

Arm

Leg

Mitten

Leg

Boot

Boot

152

BORDERS OF SQUARES

The quilts pictured from left to right are Sammarbeid Er Bare Glede
(Work Together is Always a Joy), Basket of Memories and Serenity.

FOUR PATCH & NINE PATCH BORDERS

Determine the length of borders needed. Divide that measurement by one of the following numbers listed below. This will tell you the size and number of squares you need. If necessary, try a few different numbers to get the closest measurement needed. An extension border will also help to make a border fit.

Numbers: (for finished size blocks)

3/4=.75	2 = 2
I=I	2 1/4" = 2.25
1 1/8 = 1.875	2 1/2 = 2.5
1 1/4 = 1.25	3 = 3
1 1/2 = 1.5	

Alternative: If you need a size not listed, decide what size you need and add 1/2" for the seam allowance. (1/4" on all sides = 1/2")

The block sizes include 1/4" seam allowance

Finished size:

A: 3/4" = cut 1.25" squares

B: 1" = cut 1.5" squares

C: 1 1/8" = cut 1 5/8" squares

D: 1 1/4" = cut 1 3/4" squares

E: 1 1/2" = cut 2" squares

F: 2" = cut 2 1/2" squares

G: 2 1/4" = cut 2 3/4" squares

H: 2 1/2" = cut 3" squares

I: 3" = cut 3 1/2" squares

FOUR PATCH:

Sew two squares together. Press the seam allowances towards one side. Sew two more squares together and press in the opposite direction of the first unit. Sew the two units together. Make the required number of units and sew together.

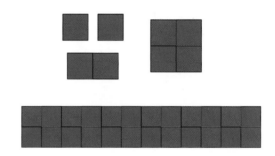

NINE PATCH:

Sew three squares together. Press the seam allowance towards one side. Repeat the process and press the seams in the opposite direction of the first unit. Repeat and press the seams in the opposite direction of unit 2. Sew the three units together.

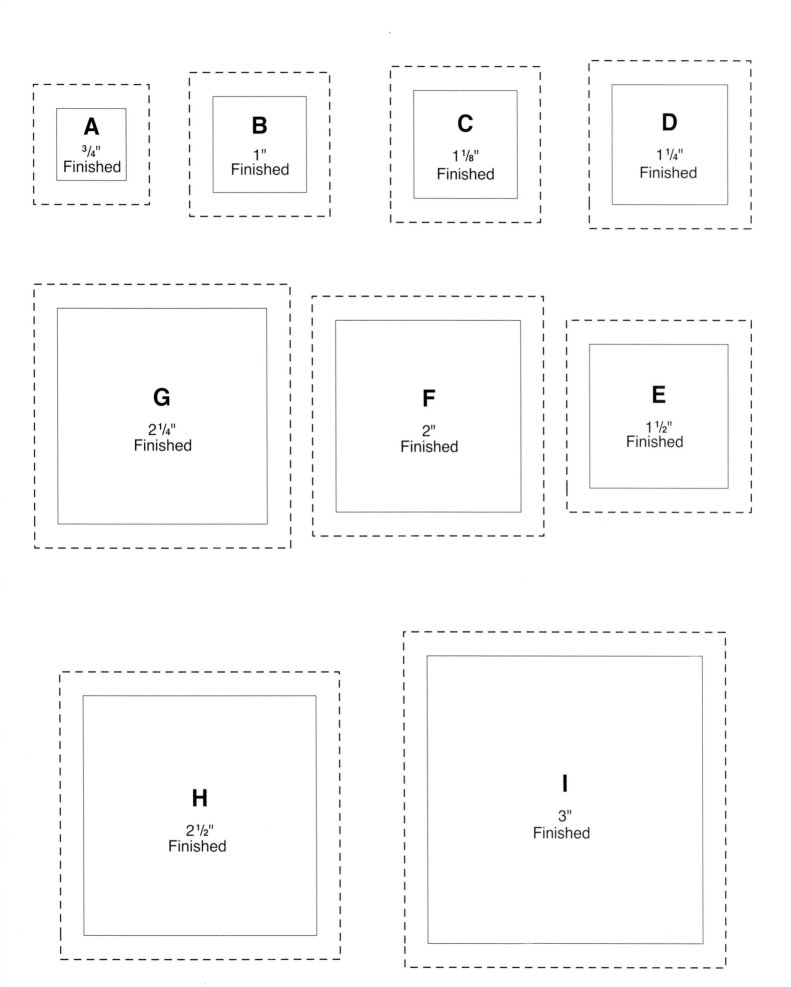

WINTER PATH

Finishes 1 3/4" x desired length

Measurements include 1/4" seam allowance.

Determine how long you would like your borders to be____. Divide that number by
1.75____.
This will let you know how many squares you will need.
Cutting Guide:

      Row 1: cut random numbers of 1 1/2" squares.

      Row 2: cut random numbers of 1 1/2" x 1 1/4" rectangles.

There isn't any real layout to this border. Arrange the squares for row 1 in a way that
appeals to you and sew them together. Press all of the seams towards one direction.
Do the same for row 2. Press the seams in the opposite direction of row 1.
Sew the two rows together.

Sew the borders to the hanging.

LOG CABIN BORDER

Measurements include 1/4" seam allowance.

Determine the length of the borders needed. Divide that number by 2.5 or 3.75_____.
This will give you the size and number of blocks needed.

2 1/2" (finished size) Log Cabin Blocks - (requirements for each block.)

Center Fabric: Template A: cut 1 1/2" x 1 1/2" square.

Light Fabric: A: cut 1 1/2" x 1 1/2" square.

        B: cut 1 1/2" x 2" rectangle

        C: cut 1 1/2" x 2 1/2" rectangle

        D: cut 1 1/2" x 3" rectangle

Dark Fabric: B: cut 1 1/2" x 2" rectangle

        C: cut 1 1/2" x 2 1/2" rectangle

        D: cut 1 1/2" x 3" rectangle

        E: cut 1 1/2" x 3 1/2" rectangle

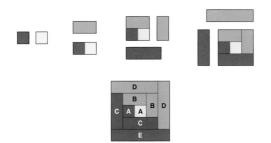

Option: Instead of the log cabin blocks, you may choose to use four 2 1/2" squares in the corners of the borders.

3 3/4" (finished size) Log Cabin Blocks - (requirements for each block.)

Center Fabric: Template F: cut 1 1/4" x 1 1/4" square

Dark Fabric: F: cut 1 1/4" x 1 1/4" square.

        G: cut 1 1/4" x 2" rectangle

        H: cut 1 1/4" x 2 3/4" rectangle

        I: cut 1 1/4" x 3 1/4" rectangle

Light Fabric: G: cut 1 1/4" x 2" rectangle

        H: cut 1 1/4" x 2 3/4" rectangle

        I: cut 1 1/4" x 3 1/2" rectangle

        J: cut 1 1/4" x 4 3/4" rectangle

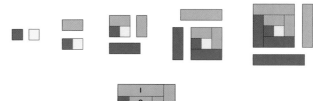

Option: Instead of the log cabin blocks, you may choose to use four 3 3/4" squares in the border corners.

Piece according to the diagram. Press the seams as you go. There are many layouts for log cabin blocks. Play around with the blocks until you find the layout that best suits your hanging.

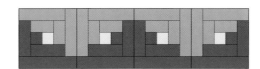

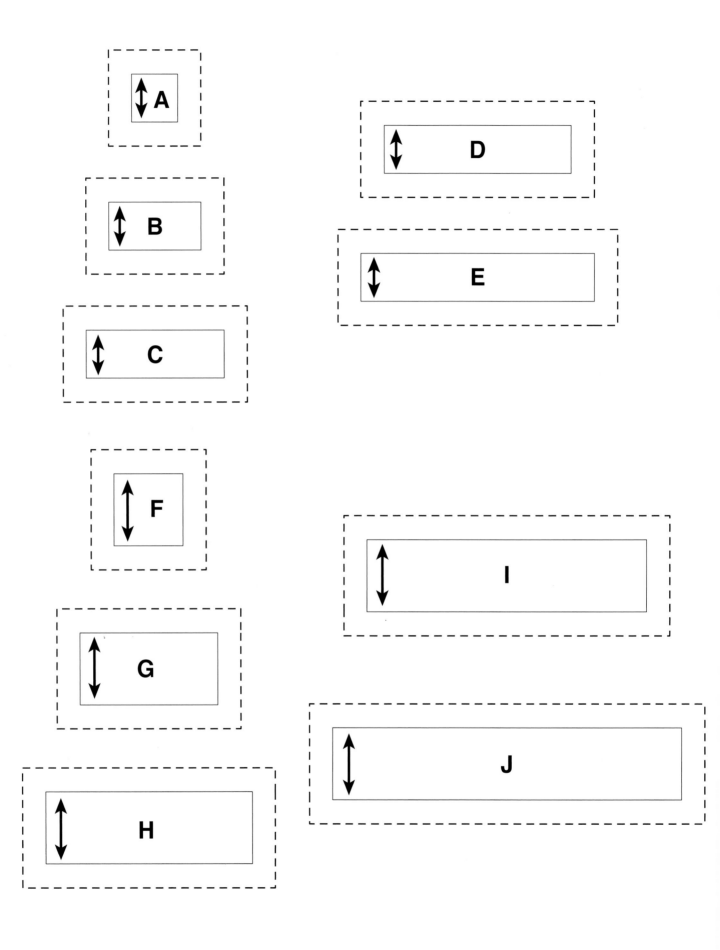

IRISH CHAIN BORDER

Finished 4 1/4" wide x the desired length

Measurements include 1/4" seam allowance

Determine the length of borders needed. Divide that measurement by 4.25_____.

This will tell you how many blocks are needed for the borders.

You may need to add an extension border to the hanging to make the border fit.

Multiply the number of blocks needed by how many template pieces you need for 1 block.

This will tell you how many of each template piece you will need to cut.

Cutting directions:

For each block you will need the following:

Chain fabric:

Template A: cut 3 -1 1/2" squares.

Chain background fabric:

Template A: cut 2 - 1 1/2" squares

Template B: cut 2 rectangles 1 1/2" x 2 1/2"

Triangle fabric

Template C: cut 5 1/2" squares and cut in half twice on the diagonal.

This will yield 4 triangles per square.

Template D: cut 4" squares and cut in half once on the diagonal.

This will yield 2 triangles per square.

Assemble according to the diagram.

Pressing: when making the Irish chain block, press the fabric towards the chain fabric. After you have pieced the triangles to the Irish chain block, press towards the triangles.

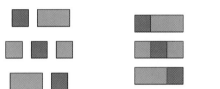

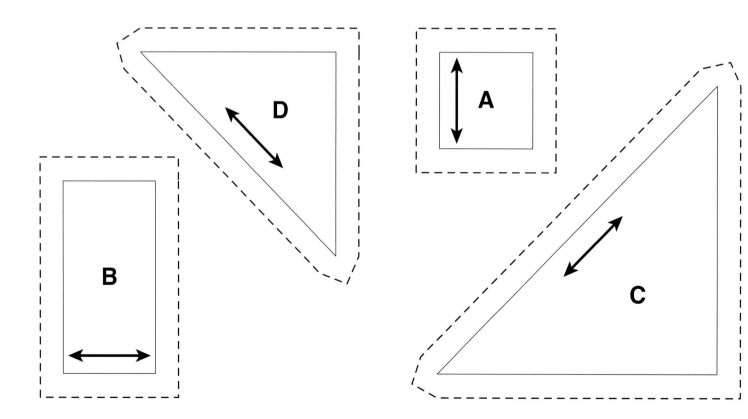

SQUARE IN A SQUARE

All seam allowances included in figures.

Determine the length of the borders needed. Divide by either 3 or 4. This will tell you which size square to use and how many you will need for each border.

The following will make 1 block.

3" finished block:

Template A: cut two 2 3/8" squares. Cut the squares in half once on the diagonal.

Template B: cut one 2 1/2" square.

4" finished block:

Template D: cut one 3 1/4" square.

Template E: cut two 2 7/8" squares. Cut the squares in half once on the diagonal.

Sew a triangle onto the square on opposing sides. Press towards the square. Sew the other triangles to the remaining sides and press.

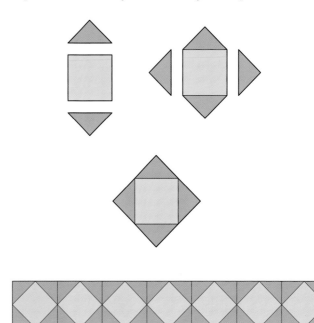

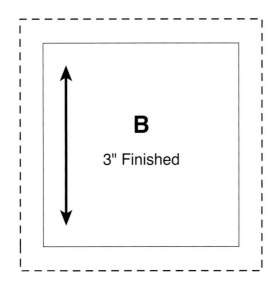

B

3" Finished

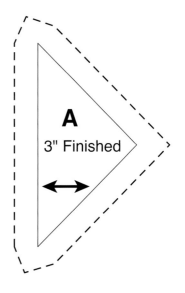

A

3" Finished

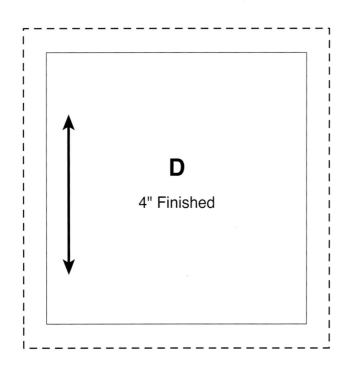

D

4" Finished

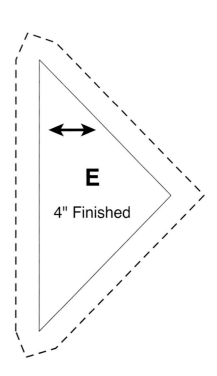

E

4" Finished

BORDERS OF CHOICE

Sammarbeid Er Bare Glede
(Work Together is Always a Joy)

Rebecca's Flowers

Star in Bloom

MIDNIGHT STAR BORDER

Finished border 5" x the desired length

Measurements include 1/4" seam allowance.

Each star unit finishes 5" x 7 1/2"

For each star you will need the following:

Star Points: Template A: cut 8

Star Center: Template C: cut 1

Star Background: Template B: cut 4

Star Background Corners: Template C: cut 20

Sewing directions:

Sew star point A to B and press towards the star point. Sew the other star point to the other side of B. Press towards the star point. Make 28 units.

Side Stars: Sew the star points to the top and bottom of four star centers. Press the seam allowance towards the center. Sew the corner squares to each end of four star points. Sew to one side of the star. Press the seam allowance towards the center.

Borders between the stars:

Determine the length of border needed. From this measurement subtract

13_____.

Divide by 2 _____ and add .5 _____.

Cut eight pieces of two different fabrics 3" wide by the above measurement.

Sew the borders together so you have eight sets.

Press the seam allowance towards the dark fabric.

Sew the border strips to each end of the side stars.

Press the seam allowance towards the border.

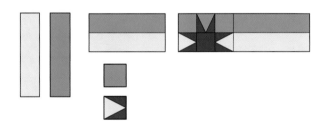

Sew a corner square to one end of each of four star points. Sew these star points to the end of the plain borders. Sew to the top and bottom of the hanging.

Corner Stars: Sew star points to the top and bottom of four star centers. Press the seam allowance towards the center. Sew the corner squares to each end of four star points. Press the seam allowance towards the center. Sew to one side of the star. Press the seam allowance towards the center. Sew the corner star units to the ends of the remaining borders.

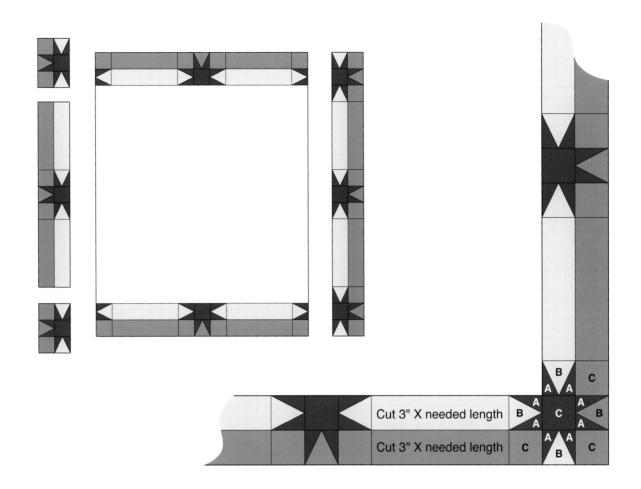

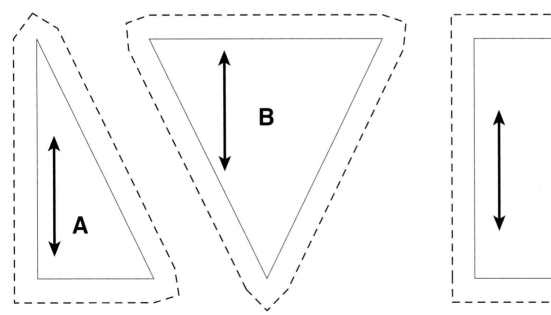

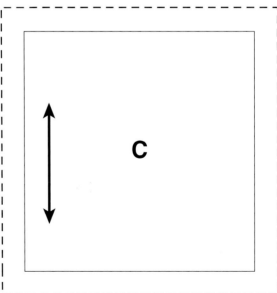

Cut 3" X needed length

Cut 3" X needed length

A

B

C

SCRAPPY RECTANGLES BORDER

3 3/4" x desired length

Measurements include 1/4" seam allowance.

Cutting Guide:

Cut the first plain border 2" x desired length.

Cut the second plain border 2 1/4" x desired length.

Rectangles: cut the fabric 1 3/8" x various widths between 1 1/2" and 2 3/4". Randomly sew these pieces together until you have the desired length. Press all of the seam allowances towards the same side.

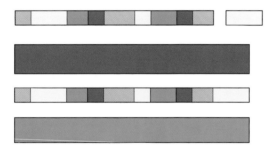

Sew the rectangle border between the two plain borders.

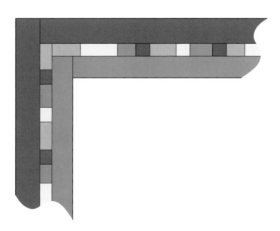

CURVY PATH

Cutting Requirements:

      Green fabric: templates A, B, C

      Mauve fabric: templates D, E

Covered Cording:

Cover narrow cording with bias strips that have been sewn together. Use a zipper foot and sew the covered cording to pieces D and E, sewing raw edge to raw edge. Fold the raw edges towards the back and press. Place these borders on top of the green borders. Carefully topstitch next to the cording. Sew piece E to A and piece E to C. Sew to the hanging. Next sew piece D to B. Sew the borders to the hanging.

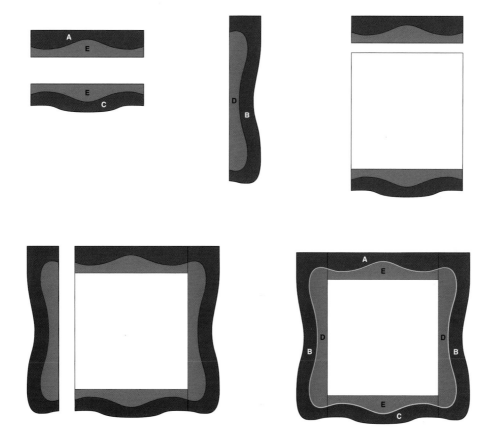

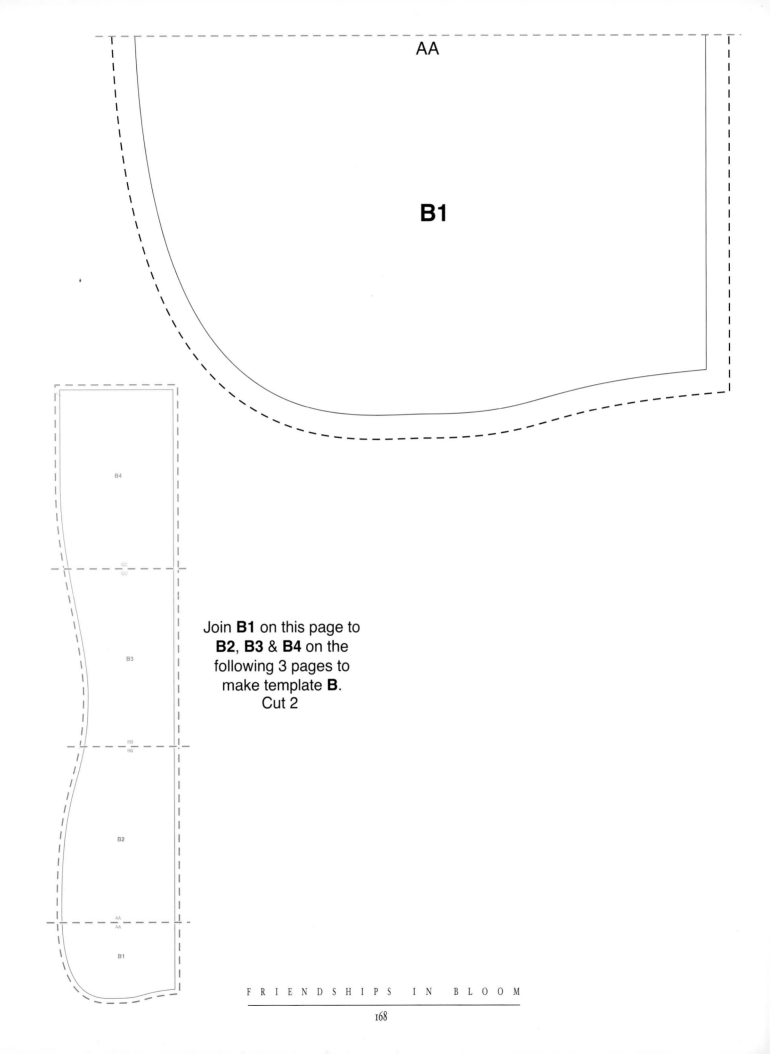

AA

B1

Join **B1** on this page to **B2**, **B3** & **B4** on the following 3 pages to make template **B**.
Cut 2

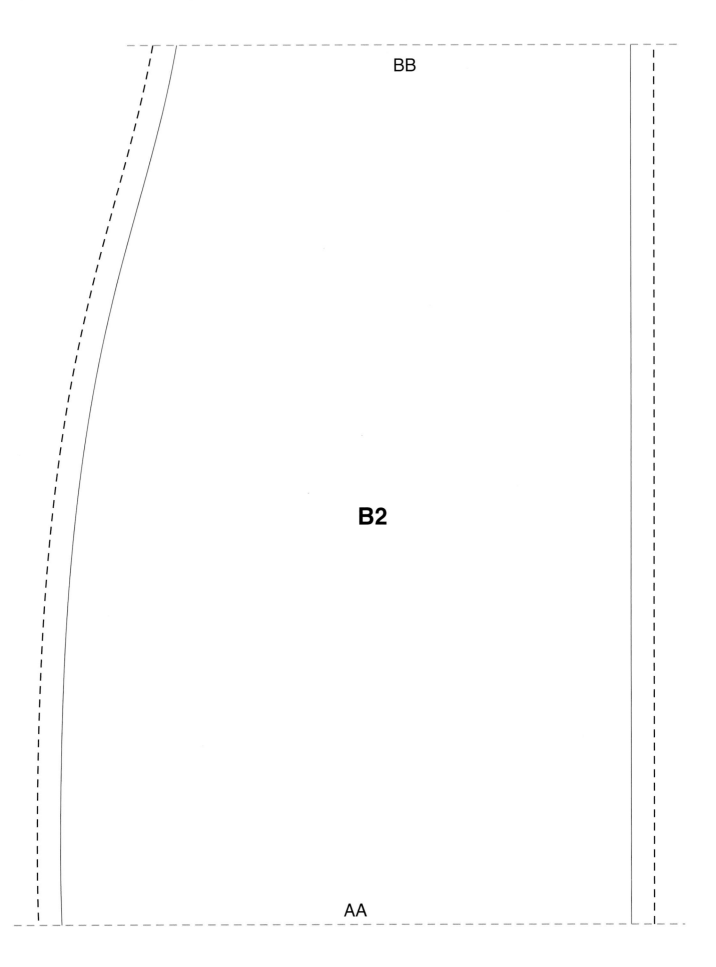

BB

B2

AA

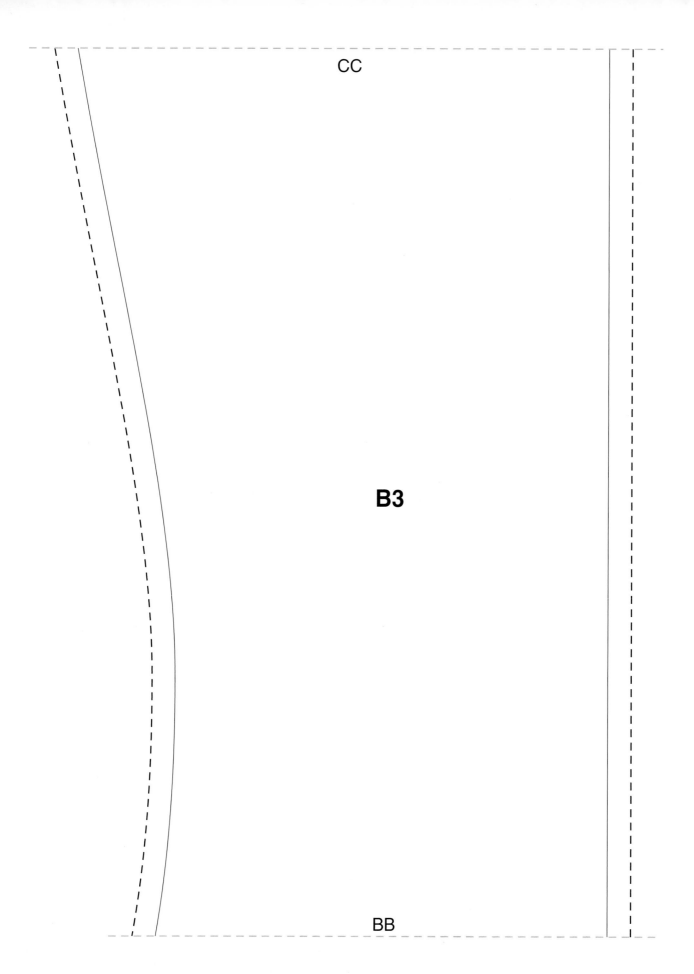

CC

B3

BB

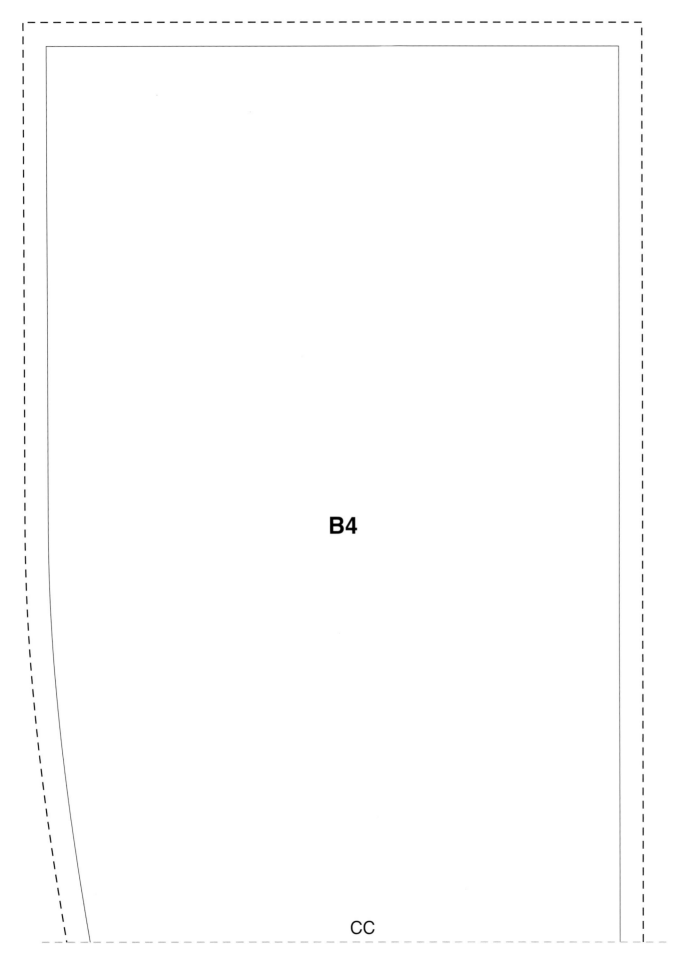

B4

CC

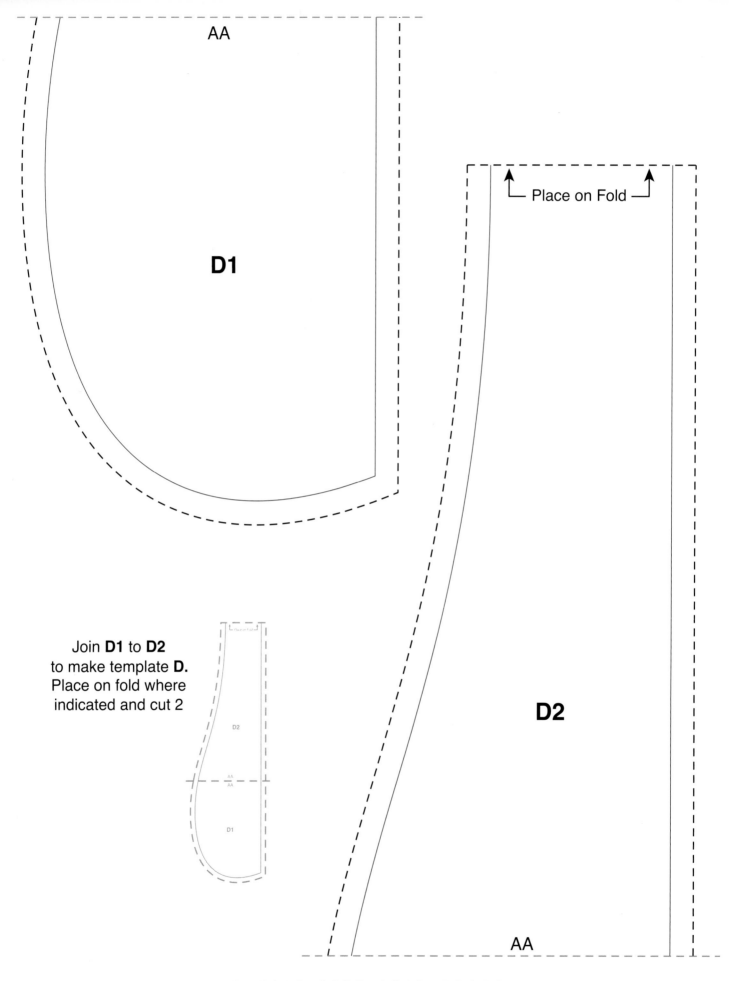

AA

D1

Place on Fold

Join **D1** to **D2**
to make template **D.**
Place on fold where
indicated and cut 2

D2

AA

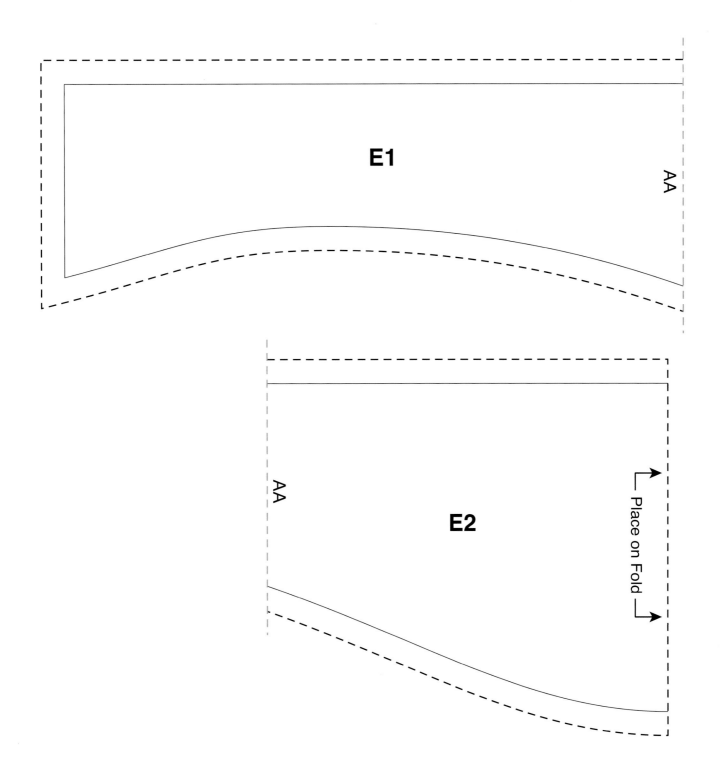

E1

AA

AA

E2

Place on Fold

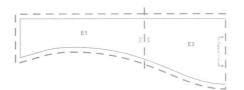

Join **E1** to **E2**
to make template **E.**
Place on fold where
indicated and cut 2

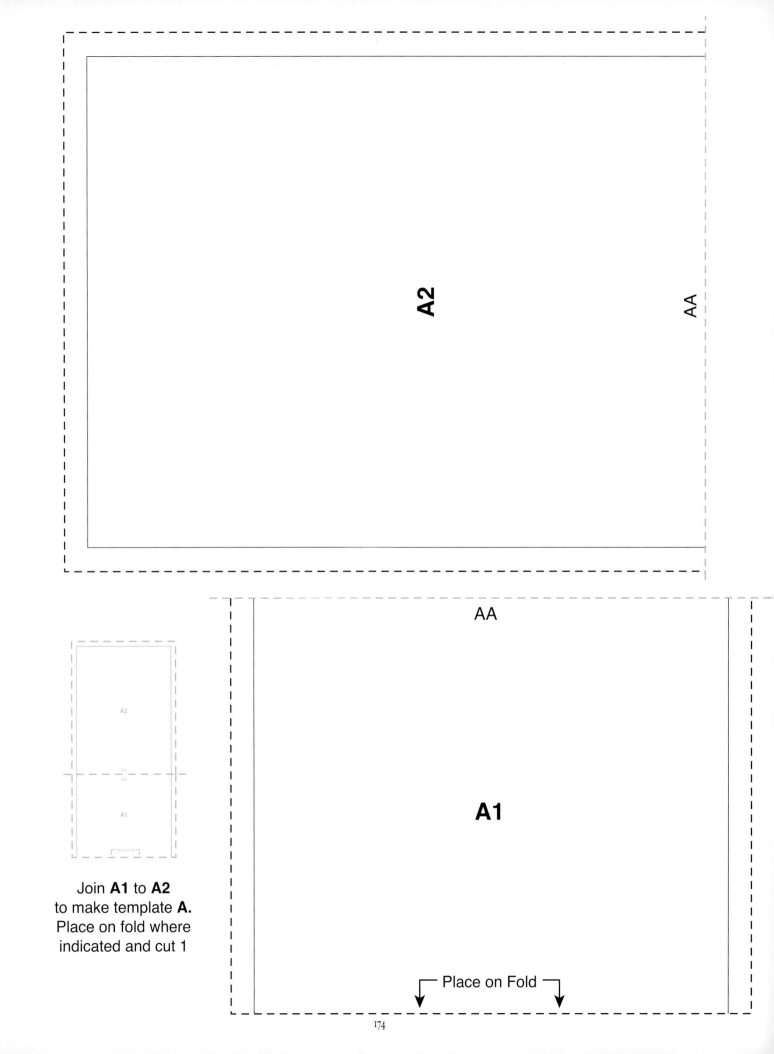

A2

AA

AA

A1

Join **A1** to **A2**
to make template **A.**
Place on fold where
indicated and cut 1

⌐ Place on Fold ⌐

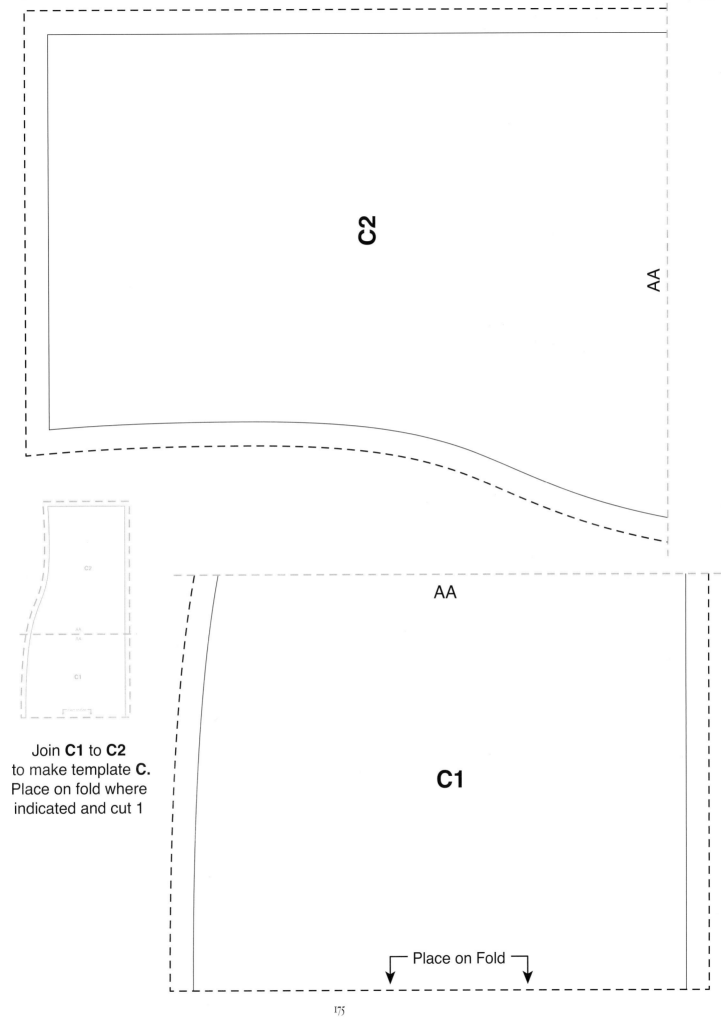

C2

AA

AA

Join **C1** to **C2**
to make template **C.**
Place on fold where
indicated and cut 1

C1

← Place on Fold →

SNAIL'S TRAIL BORDER

Finishes 6" x desired length

Measurements include 1/4" seam allowance.

Press the seams towards the triangles.

Cutting Requirements:

Yellow/Green/Red/Blue

Template A: cut 4 of each color

Template B: cut 4 of each color

Template D: cut 4 of each color

Template E: cut 4 of each color

Border Fabric: cut 6 1/2" x desired length

Sew the yellow A to the yellow/green side.

Sew the red A to the blue/red side.

Press the seams towards the triangles.

Sew the blue A to the blue/yellow side.

Sew the green A to the green/blue side.

Press the seams towards the triangles.

Piecing Guide:

Sew yellow C to blue C. Press seam allowances towards the yellow. Sew green C to red C. Press seam allowances towards the blue. Sew these units together.

Sew the green D to the top of the green/blue squares.

Sew the blue D to the bottom of the yellow/blue squares.

Press the seams towards the triangles.

Sew the yellow D to the green/yellow side.

Sew the red D to the red/blue side.

Press the seams towards the triangles.

Sew the blue E to the blue/yellow side.

Sew the green E to the red/green side.

Press the seams towards the triangles.

Sew the red E to the blue/red sides.

Sew the yellow E to the yellow/green side.

Press the seams towards the triangles.

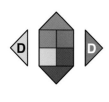

Sew the yellow B to the yellow/green side

Sew the red B to the blue/red side.

Press the seams towards the triangles.

Sew the blue B to the yellow/blue side.

Sew the green B to the green/red side.

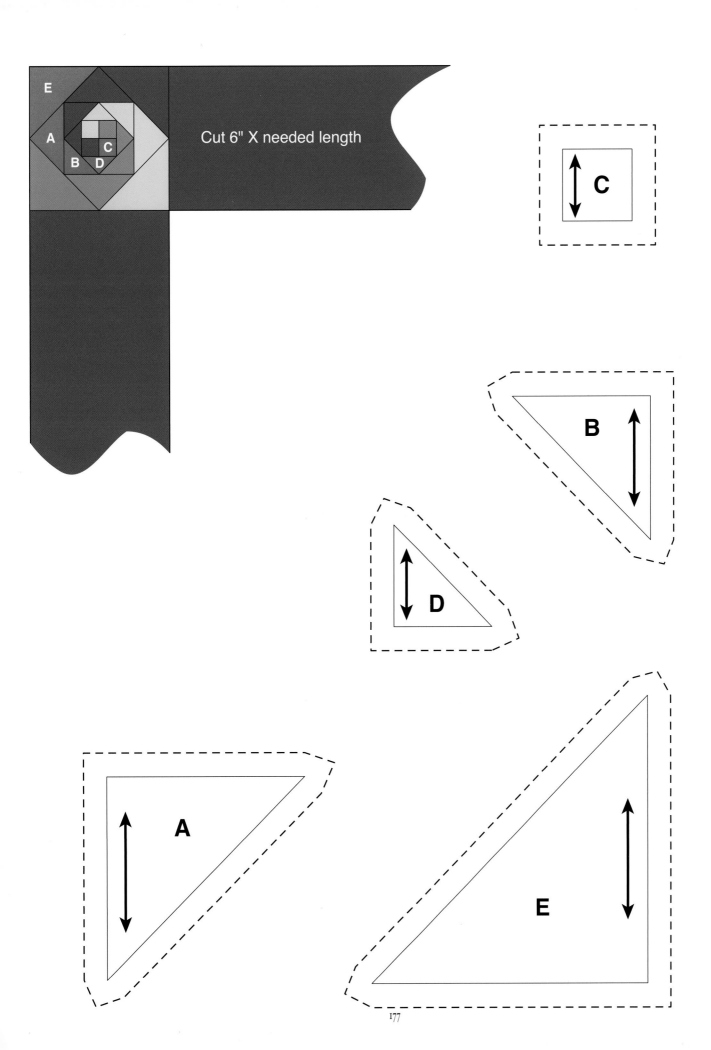

Cut 6" X needed length

E

A

B D

C

C

B

D

A

E

PRAIRIE POINT BORDER

Finished Size: 3" by the desired length

Measurements include 1/4" seam allowance

Determine the length of the border needed.

Cut the border background 3 1/2" wide by the desired length.

Prairie Points: cut 6 1/2" squares. The number of squares needed may vary. Decide if you want the prairie points spaced randomly or if you want them to fill the entire length of the border.

Fold a square in half on the diagonal and press. Fold in half again on the diagonal and press.

Place and sew as desired on border.

Alternative: Smaller squares will yield smaller, delicate prairie points. You may want to experiment with different size squares and border widths.

BASKET IN THE CORNERS BORDER

Finished: 3 1/2" x desired length

Measurements include 1/4" seam allowance.

Determine how long the borders need to be. Cut 4 borders 4" by this measurement.

Basket corners: (cutting four baskets)

Basket fabric: Template A: cut four

                      Template D: cut eight

Background fabric: Template C: cut eight

                      Template B: cut four

                      Template A: cut four

Sew C and D together. Press the seams towards C.

Sew basket piece A to background piece A. Press the seams towards the darker fabric.

Sew the C/D unit to the A/A unit. Press the seams towards the basket.

Sew B to the bottom of basket unit. Press the seams towards B.

Sew the plain borders to the hanging.

Sew the four basket units to each end of two borders. Press and sew to the hanging.

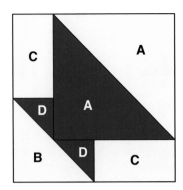

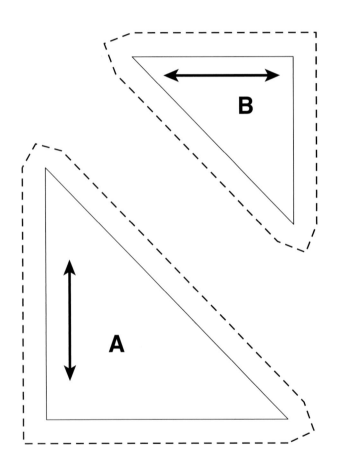

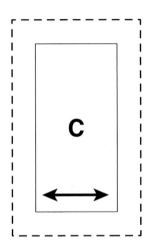

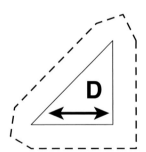

MARINER'S STARS BORDER

Finishes 4 1/2" x desired length

Measurements include 1/4" seam allowance

Cutting instructions: cut the plain border 4 3/4" wide by the desired length. Sew the borders to the hanging.

Mariner's Stars:

        Template A: cut twelve

        Piece B: cut sixteen rectangles 1 1/2" x 3"

        Piece C: cut thirty-two squares 3" x 3"

Make sixteen of pattern D which is paper pieced. Make 16 copies of the pattern.

Paper Piecing Instructions:

1. With your fingers, make a crease in the paper along the sewing line between piece number 1 and piece number 2. Turn the paper over so the blank side of the pattern is facing you. Feel for the crease you made. Place the first fabric right side up. Place the next piece of fabric with right side facing the first fabric. (The back of fabric number 2 should be facing you.) While holding the fabric in place, turn the paper over. The printed side should be facing you and the fabric should be underneath the paper. Sew on the dotted line. Trim the seam allowance to 1/4." Press the fabric so both right sides are facing you. Make a crease where the next sewing line is. Place the next fabric so the wrong side is facing you. Turn it over and sew on the dotted line.

2. After you are finished, trim the sections down to a 1/4" seam allowance along the outside edges. Sew piece A between the sections as shown. Carefully tear the paper off the back. Appliqué the Mariner's Stars to the background.

Smaller Appliqué Stars: Template M: cut twenty-four

        Template N: cut eight

Appliqué piece N to the background. Place the M pieces in the center of N as shown and appliqué.

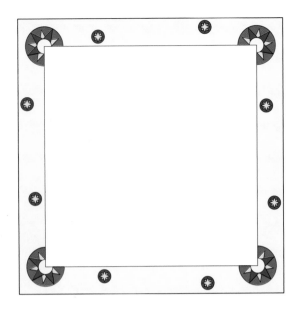

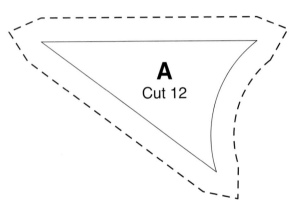

A
Cut 12

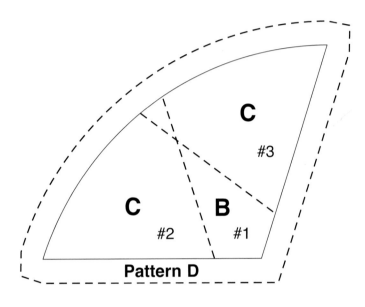

C

C

B

#3

#2

#1

Pattern D

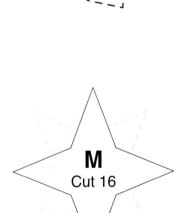

M
Cut 16

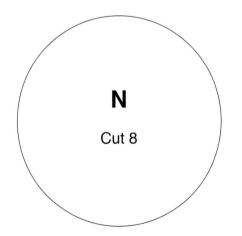

N
Cut 8

CACTUS FLOWER BORDER

Finished size: 2 1/2" x desired length

Measurements include 1/4" seam allowance.

Determine how long you would like your border to be.

Cut four borders 3" by this measurement.

Cactus Flower: cutting for four blocks.

    Background fabric: Template A: cut 4

                  Template D: cut 8

    Cactus Flower: Template B: cut 16

    Cactus Flower Bottom: Template C: cut 4

Piecing Guide: sew template B to D. Press the seams open. Make eight units. Sew B to the other side of this unit. Press the seams open.

Sew A to the side as shown. Press the seams open. Sew the other diamond unit to this one. Press the seams open. Sew piece C to the bottom of the cactus flowers. Press the seams towards C.

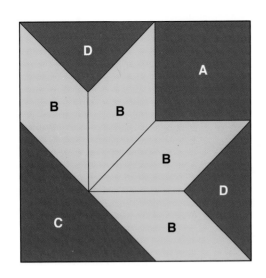

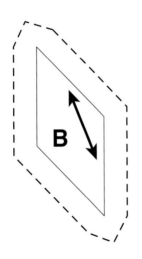

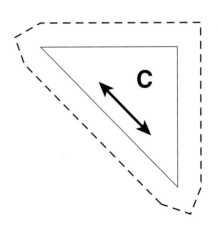

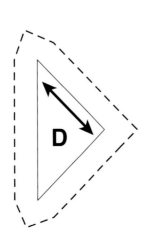

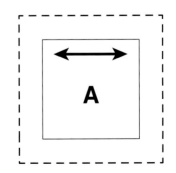